To Col. Dave Murray,

My XO & personal hero! As you head back to the _real_ Air Force, enjoy a book about _real_ pilots!

Thanks for your help & support.

Good Luck & Semper Fi,

Tom Thaler
Col USMC

Corsairs and Flattops

Marine Carrier Air Warfare, 1944–1945

Corsairs and Flattops

JOHN POMEROY CONDON

NAVAL INSTITUTE PRESS
ANNAPOLIS, MARYLAND

LIBRARY OF CONGRESS CATALOGING-IN-PUBLICATION DATA

    Corsairs and flattops : Marine carrier air warfare, 1944–1945 / John
Pomeroy Condon.
        p.   cm.
    Includes index.
    ISBN 1-55750-127-0 (alk. paper) : $27.95
    1. World War, 1939–1945—Aerial operations, American. 2. United
States. Navy—Aviation. I. Title.
    D790.C656   1997
    940.54'25—dc21   97-31406

Printed in the United States of America on acid-free paper ∞
05 04 03 02 01 00 99 98   9 8 7 6 5 4 3 2
First printing

FRONTISPIECE: Air Group 4 is ready to launch in the South China Sea
on 12 January 1945, with Corsairs of VMF-124 and VMF-213 in the
foreground. (U.S. NAVY PHOTO)

Contents

■ VI

Contents

Foreword

Predicting the total impact of a military decision has seldom been done with any accuracy. Historically, this inability to predict has resulted in significant costs and even loss of the battle. Those who have been provided with the lessons learned from such events have the moral responsibility to ensure that the mistakes are not repeated on their watch.

In *Corsairs and Flattops,* John Condon has presented us with some lessons learned the hard way that are as applicable today as they were in 1944. He has meticulously documented the reasons why naval aviation must maintain the ability to swing forces afloat to meet operational requirements and should, therefore, carefully consider a decision to limit carrier training for any naval aviator. His concern is for the people who must execute the orders. The term he uses is "had to be accepted." He is referring to the situation where the Marines were not properly trained and, in some cases, not properly equipped for the mission they had to accept. Why were they not ready? From the carrier operations standpoint it was because priority had been given to Navy squadrons who were responding to the requirements of the Pacific War and were also operating under difficult training circumstances. Essentially no deck time was allotted to Marine aviators going through flight training, and little after they reached the operational forces. This lack of any basic carrier training, coupled with the urgency of the situation and, in some part, due to the Corsairs carrier suitability, resulted in tragic loss of life and equipment. Most of these losses were operational, not combat. Today we would classify them as occurring during the administrative part of the hop. Not only were the Marines lacking in carrier experience, they were also weak in navigation and instrument flying skills. Throw in some bad weather, and you have all the ingredients for a disaster.

It is a credit to those involved, the author included, that the mission was successfully accomplished. The price tag was exceedingly high, but they did it. The courage, innovativeness, and determination of the individuals involved have provided one of the greatest chapters in naval aviation history and, as we say, was in keeping with the highest traditions of the naval service.

Marine squadrons are on board carriers today at a rate that is higher than at any time since World War II. They are performing splendidly, in part because they were properly prepared for the mission. They received their introduction to carrier operations in flight school, and the leadership in both the Navy and Marine Corps saw to it that they received the required follow-on training. This is the message that General Condon is sending. Training can and must be done properly. In times of stress, as was the case during the war in Vietnam, we again cut Marines out of the carrier pipeline during flight training and later sent them to sea where the first time they saw a carrier was over the nose of a Crusader or a Phantom. We ignored the lesson learned.

Today's leadership seems well attuned to this requirement, but we also have the benefit of peacetime operations. It is when the unexpected occurs and we start making the hard decisions that we need to remember the words of this great Marine aviator. He has provided us with a knowledgeable discussion, easy to read, that was written from the heart. For this, naval aviators are in his debt.

Happy landings, General.

GEN. J. R. DAILEY, USMC (Ret.)

Acknowledgments

In an attempt to make the 1944–45 versions of the eighteen Marine carrier squadrons "come alive" again fifty years later, some fifty members of those units were contacted. The request was for anecdotes and pictures mainly, and the response was outstanding. Each unit of the eighteen was represented, and individuals "networked" the project widely for a super return. It would be difficult to mention all of the respondents, but the principal ones included Brig. Gen. H. W. Hise, Col. W. R. Campbell, Brig. Gen. W. A. Millington, Lt. Col. O. K. Williams, Col. Archie J. Clapp, Lt. Col. J. P. Golden, Lt. Col. C. P. Weiland, Col. Warner O. Chapman, Brig. Gen. George E. Dooley, Col. Vernon H. Salisbury, Col. James E.

Swett, Col. Herbert H. Long, Maj. Albert G. Schoneberger, Col. Richard W. Johnson, Capt. James L. Secrest, Col. Roland E. Spjeldet, Capt. John E. Worlund, Lt. Col. Charles E. McLean, Lt. Col. Ernest A. Buford, Lt. Col. Thomas O. Bales, Capt. Edward J. Montagne, Mr. Bob Woolfe, and Mr. Terry Lynch, all USMC or USMCR (Ret.).

In bringing together the fifty responses of this great list, I was given a major assist by Mr. Dan Crawford and his staff of the Reference Section of the Marine Corps Historical Center, and by the Operational Archives Section of the Navy Historical Center, particularly by the director, Mr. Bernard F. Cavalcante and archivist Mr. Mike Walker. Archivist Frederick J. Graboske of the Marine Corps Historical Center and his staff were constantly helpful over the two-year effort to bring this complex story to completion, especially the personal papers collection under Ms. Amy Cantin and her volunteer assistant, Col. James Leon, USMC (Ret.).

The principal textual sources consulted were *Victory and Occupation*, volume V of *History of U.S. Marine Corps Operations in World War II*, by Benis M. Frank and Henry I. Shaw, Jr.; *History of Marine Corps Aviation in World War II* by Robert Sherrod; Rear Adm. Samuel Eliot Morison's *A History of United States Naval Operations in World War II*, vols. XIII and XIV; Adm. Frederick C. Sherman's *Combat Command: The American Aircraft Carriers in the Pacific War*; and the records of the Marine and Navy squadrons concerned, as filed in the National Archives.

Corsairs and Flattops

1   The Mission

From the mid-1920s, Marine squadrons qualified on board fleet carriers from time to time as part of their mission, as it was then defined. Such operations began with the first carrier, the converted collier USS *Langley*, but were somewhat spasmodic in nature rather than being a regular part of the annual training schedule. Carrier operations received much more emphasis from the West Coast Marine squadrons—based at the North Island naval air station in San Diego, the very hub of Pacific Fleet carrier operations—than they received in Quantico, Virginia, where the East Coast Marine squadrons were primarily based.

In terms of mission definition and refinement, as well as annual squadron training, one of the greatest advances for

Marine Corps aviation stemmed from an important assignment during the early 1930s. In 1931 two Marine scouting
squadrons in San Diego were assigned to operate as compo-
nent units of Pacific Fleet carriers for a period of almost three
years. The two squadrons were assigned to Aircraft, Battle
Force, Pacific Fleet and ordered to the *Lexington* (CV 2) and
Saratoga (CV 3). Scouting Squadron 15-M, commanded by
Capt. William O. Brice, reported aboard *Lexington,* and Scouting Squadron 14-M, under Capt. William J. Wallace, aboard
Saratoga, both on 2 November 1931.

Prior to this assignment, Marine squadrons had been
somewhat loosely controlled with respect to doctrine and a
specific annual training regimen. During the three years that
the two squadrons operated day in and day out under the
Navy, however, about 60 percent of the active duty Marine
pilots rotated through the two units. Their valuable experience was soon transmitted to all squadrons of the Fleet Marine Force on both coasts.

First Lt. (later Brig. Gen.) Edward C. Dyer was one of the
earliest to gain this expertise and know-how. He evaluated
the experience as:

. . . a rude awakening. . . . There was no monkey business whatsoever. In the first place, we were handed a doctrine, a book, a
guide, that told us how the squadron should be organized. . . . we
had a commanding officer, an executive officer, a flight officer, an
engineering officer, a materiel officer, and so on, and the duties of
each officer were all spelled out. . . . The organization and operation of the squadron was definitely controlled. The aircraft were
issued by the Air Battle Force materiel people. They would . . .
give us the airplanes; we would then have to maintain them. But
these fellows would arrive and inspect. . . . just to see if you were
maintaining them in a satisfactory condition. . . . All our material
was requisitioned and accounted for. . . . We had so many hours
of gunnery . . . navigation . . . radio practice . . . formation flying
. . . night flying . . . and we jolly well had to do it.

The spread of this type of disciplined syllabus training
under a clearly defined mission was the foundation for the

operational stature of Marine Corps aviation in the years immediately prior to Pearl Harbor. It was a true evolutionary milestone.

On 18 January 1939, the secretary of the navy refined the mission and organization of U.S. Marine Corps aviation as follows:

Marine Corps Aviation is to be equipped, organized and trained primarily for the support of the Fleet Marine Force in landing operations and in support of troop activities in the field; and secondarily as replacement squadrons for carrier-based naval aircraft;

The organization, personnel complements, and other details of Marine Corps aviation are to conform as closely as practicable to similar naval aviation organizations;

The Bureau of Aeronautics is to exercise supervision over their respective activities connected with Marine Corps aviation in the manner provided for similar naval aviation units.

The sudden shock of Pearl Harbor and the beginning of World War II in the Pacific was monumentally traumatic. For Marine Corps air, it meant that virtually all carrier operations came to an abrupt halt. From 1942 until late in 1944, carrier training for deploying Marine Corps squadrons was extremely limited. The demand for carrier decks was so strong in order to meet fleet operational requirements, that carrier training for Marine units was essentially nonexistent. During this period only minimal training for deck launches and catapult shots from very small transport carriers could be made available. Of the rapidly growing number of Marine pilots who completed flight training by mid-1944—approaching a total of ten thousand—only a minute percentage had ever been on board a carrier.

Early 1944 saw the demise of the Japanese in the south Pacific and southwest Pacific operations areas and the start of the major Allied offensives through the central Pacific and the Philippines toward the Japanese home islands. Ultimate victory was still far off, but was becoming recognizable in the vague distance. This was a great improvement over the dismal outlook of the immediate post–Pearl Harbor days and much of 1942. Changes in the conduct of the war in the Pacific during 1944 had some very direct effects on Marine Corps aviation overall, but particularly on employment of Marine air on carriers.

As the Solomons campaign was brought to a successful conclusion early in 1944, the bloody central Pacific campaign was well under way. However, the distances in the central Pacific were far greater than those of the convenient "stepping stones" of the Solomons campaign. In fact they were of such magnitude as to make it infeasible for Marine air to meet its primary mission of "the support of the Fleet Marine Force in landing operations and in support of troop activities in the field," unless it was operating from carriers. Furthermore, analyses of the Navy air support of the Marines at Tarawa in late November 1943 showed inadequacies compared to that rendered by Marine air units in the Solomons.

As a result of these problems, Lt. Gen. Holland M. Smith recommended after Tarawa that "consideration be given to the assignment of at least one Marine Aircraft Wing specifically for direct support in landing operations." However, the judgment of the Navy high command in early 1944 was that carrier deck availability was still not sufficient to meet fleet demands. Thus the Marine carrier program did not get approved and organized until very late in the fall of 1944. Only three Marine carrier air groups (MCVGs) would deploy prior to V-J Day, with a fourth arriving in the combat area the day the war ended.

Other events led to a separate branch of Marine carrier operations. By the fall of 1944, the losses inflicted on the Japanese air forces in the southern Pacific areas were of such magnitude that the Japanese high command was forced to make marked changes in tactics. It increasingly resorted to the use of suicide attacks on Allied combat shipping. At first this was on a random basis and not well defined as to objectives with respect to ship types. But as the Japanese situation continued to worsen, it became very clear that the intention was to largely use the kamikaze tactic against key capital ships.

The Allied defensive counter to this enemy effort was to raise the quantity and performance of the fighters in the fleet carrier air groups. Increased fighter numbers would make it possible to keep more fighters on patrol over the task forces at any given time. Greater fighter speed and rate of climb would enhance the ability of the combat air patrol (CAP) to get the kamikazes before they could reach their target.

While both overall fighter numbers and improved performance were deemed essential, the latter was far more difficult to achieve quickly. Advanced fighters were too far down the production schedules to fill the immediate demand for better performance. War planners thus began looking for a carrier-capable fighter that had better performance than the F6F Hellcat, which had been chosen by the Navy as the standard fighter for fleet carriers in early 1943. Attention was directed to the F4U Corsair as a possible solution. It was generally accepted that the Corsair had about twenty knots of speed on the Hellcat and about an eight hundred foot per minute better rate of climb. These superior characteristics overrode some concerns regarding the carrier suitability of the Corsair.

The Marine Corps had the good fortune of receiving the Corsair as its standard fighter when the Navy chose the Hellcat. Marine Corps aviation and the Corsair had risen to prominence in the combat annals of the nation during the Solomons campaign of 1943 and 1944. One shore-based Navy Corsair squadron, Fighting Squadron (VF) 17, shared that prominence with the Marine Corps. Another, VF-12, also shared the early struggles to get the Corsair combat-ready, but transitioned to F6Fs before that was fully accomplished.

In the national interest, the Marine Corps was asked in late 1944 to put two Corsair squadrons aboard each of five first-line *Essex* (CV 9)-class carriers of Task Forces 38 and 58 as soon as possible. The story of the Marine Corps response to this request constitutes a major portion of Marine aviation carrier operations in World War II.

■

The Marine escort aircraft carrier (CVE) experience will be described in detail in the pages to follow, as will that of the ten Corsair squadrons that operated from the five *Essex*-class carriers. Before subjecting the two segments to any detailed scrutiny, however, it is important to look at some aspects of both from the operational context of 1944–45.

At the top of the list was the fact that few Marine pilots entering the Corps after Pearl Harbor had received any facet of carrier training. By late 1944, the accelerated growth of Marine aviation and the lack of training decks resulted in the startling situation that only about one Marine pilot in fifty had ever been exposed to any carrier training. Yet a month after their assignment to the carriers of Task Force 38 in early December, several Corsair squadrons would be involved in intensive combat. Without question the lack of preparation time for most of the Corsair squadrons tapped for this high-priority mission was a major factor in the inordinate number of operational losses of both pilots and aircraft; such a result was predictable, but it was a risk that had to be accepted as part of the mission.

The anticipated early toll in operational accidents was even more severe than expected. In a little over the first week aboard, complicated by frequent instrument weather conditions, the *Essex* squadrons lost seven pilots and thirteen Corsairs—a very heavy price indeed. During this period, the *Essex* F6Fs had no similar operational losses. As one young Marine pilot phrased it, "We just can't learn navigation and carrier operations in a week as well as the Navy does in six months."

Clearly, one important difference between carrier- and land-based air operations was the fact that, flying from a carrier, the "home base" was moving while the mission was en route to and from the target. In 1945, the position-finding aids normally available today were of course nonexistent. Keeping track of the ship was largely a "plotting board" matter. Making the necessary changes to the plotted solutions as they developed during the mission was not a simple procedure in a tight cockpit. In a combat environment where unfriendly contact was a high probability at any time, it often became a "by guess and by God" proposition. Bad weather and its requirement for instrument flying and close-formation keeping added other complications. To the extent that the urgency of the assignment schedule cut into training time for these sorts of basic mission procedures, the costs could be on the high side.

There is no useful way to compare the level of difficulty faced by the Corsairs on the big carriers with that confronting the CVE Marines. While the CVE program faced many tight schedules in its organization and training, the degree of urgency overall was less demanding than that faced by the fast carrier Corsairs.

In terms of deck size, stability, ship speed (an important factor in "wind over the deck"), and aircraft-handling facilities, however, life was much tougher on a CVE than on an *Essex*-class carrier. The latter could normally give a satisfactory 25–30 knots of wind over the deck even in a calm sea with no surface wind. The 105-class CVE's top speed, on the other hand, was only 19 knots, which often had to combine with a few knots of surface wind to give sufficient wind over the deck for flight operations.

Other ship's characteristics also favored the big carrier. In deck stability (steadiness in roll and pitch), a significant edge goes to the *Essex* class over the CVE. With much greater width and length of the flight deck, the *Essex* had the ability to clear the landing area more quickly and easily, reposition the landed aircraft, or move them below to the hangar deck.

The flight deck dimensions of the two classes of carriers gave rise to a few stories along the way. One new CVE pilot returning from his first mission was low on fuel, but was told his ship had a "foul deck" (an emergency was in progress, which prevented him from landing aboard). The pilot gave an urgent report of his fuel state—by then almost on empty —and was told to land on a nearby *Essex*-class carrier. He had never seen one close up before and was more than awed by its sheer size. In response to the order, "Land aboard," the young Marine promptly shot back, "Request duty runway!"

It is important for today's readers to remember that during World War II, carrier operations were strictly "straight deck" (as opposed to the "angled deck" of modern carriers, with separate landing and takeoff areas). A barrier system separated the landing area aft from the parking area forward. The barriers were permanently rigged, remotely controlled "fences" of cable, usually two in number, that could be quickly dropped or raised. Their purpose was to prevent any landing aircraft that missed the arresting gear from plowing into the parked aircraft forward. As the sea state increased in intensity and the amplitudes of roll and pitch of the ship rose accordingly, the probability of such a serious mishap occurring increased. In a CVE, with its much smaller and narrower flight deck, the probability was intensified. In either carrier class, operations at night under such conditions were even more dangerous, but in the CVE they were definitely marginal.

In the straight-deck days, the "ball," the angled deck, and the steam catapult, to mention just a few post–World War II innovations, had not yet been invented. All landings were under the control of a landing signal officer (LSO), who was stationed on a platform at the stern, portside. The LSO, an experienced pilot, would transmit semaphore-like visual signals to the landing aircraft relative to its approach. The signals were standardized throughout the fleet and covered altitude, attitude, speed, and other approach corrections to assure a safe arrested landing. In case the LSO chose to abort the approach for any reason, there was a "wave off" signal, which was mandatory. On receiving the wave-off, the pilot would add throttle and rejoin the pattern for another approach. The pilot could also make a voluntary wave-off at any time during his approach, and it was mandatory for the pilot to wave off if at any time he lost sight of the LSO.

On a normal approach, as the LSO brought the landing

plane up to the stern of the carrier with altitude, attitude, and speed correct, he would give another mandatory signal, the "cut." The pilot would then sharply cut his throttle and land aboard, normally catching one of the first three or four arresting wires with his tailhook. When arrested, the barriers would be dropped, the pilot would quickly raise his hook, and, guided by a plane director, he would taxi out of the landing area. As soon as the recovered aircraft cleared the area, the barriers would immediately be raised and the deck would be clear for the next landing.

Additional details of the LSO-controlled approach, including definition of the various LSO signals to the landing aircraft, are described in appendix 1.

Lt. Col. William A. Millington, commanding officer of VMF-124, relates details of his shoot-down of an enemy aircraft on 3 January 1945 to Rear Adm. Frederick C. Sherman *(right)* and Capt. C. W. Wieber *(left)* on the bridge of *Essex*.

2   The First Sortie

USS *Essex* (CV 9)

COMMANDING OFFICER
Capt. Carlos W. Wieber

CARRIER AIR GROUP 4
Cdr. George O. Klinsman

MARINE FIGHTER SQUADRON 124
Lt. Col. William A. Millington

MARINE FIGHTER SQUADRON 213
Maj. David E. Marshall

The two units that would embark on the *Essex* (CV 9), Marine Fighter Squadrons (VMFs) 124 and 213, had comparable records as Corsair fighter squadrons in the Solomons campaign, having relieved each other on combat tours during 1943. Both were returned stateside as the campaign neared its end and were based on the West Coast, where they received new personnel and conducted retraining for a return to combat. After several months both units were redeployed to Hawaii to finish squadron training at MCAS Ewa.

Each squadron had a total pilot complement of twenty-seven. At the time orders for the carrier assignment were received, VMF-124 had five combat-experienced pilots from the Solomons as a leadership nucleus; VMF-213 had only three. The balance were all pilots who had completed flight training just prior to joining earlier in 1944. For the carrier mission, each unit had a complement of eighteen F4U-1D Corsair aircraft. Excluding the eight experienced pilots, average pilot time in the Corsair was approximately four hundred hours and the average age of the pilots was just over twenty.

Most combat syllabus items had been completed before coming to Hawaii, except for carrier training. Some field carrier landing practice (FCLP) had been a part of the syllabus training, but time factors of the assignment made this minimal. By the time of their departure from Ewa for *Essex*, the fifty-four pilots in the two squadrons averaged approximately twelve actual carrier landings each. Most of these were accomplished off Hawaii and San Diego in *Makassar Strait* (CVE 91), *Saratoga* (CV 3), and *Bataan* (CVL 29), and most were last-minute landings before departing Ewa to board *Essex*.

The squadrons received orders to embark in *Hollandia* (CVE 97) at Pearl Harbor in early December 1944 for transportation to Ulithi Atoll in the Caroline Islands southwest of Guam. They arrived early on Christmas day and completed transfer to *Essex* on the twenty-sixth. Having left rear echelons at MCAS Ewa, the "tailored total" in the two squadrons boarding the carrier was 54 pilots, 4 ground officers, and 120 enlisted men. Operationally, the two squadrons were handled as one thirty-six-plane squadron under Lt. Col. William A. Millington, commanding officer of VMF-124. For reports and records, the two units were administered separately under their respective commanding officers, Millington and Maj. David E. Marshall of VMF-213.

Millington reported that personnel of the ship and the air group rendered a most cordial welcome to VMF-124 and VMF-213 upon boarding *Essex*. To extend that general "welcome aboard," Rear Adm. Frederick C. Sherman, the carrier division commander whose flag was aboard *Essex*, invited

Colonel Millington into his staff mess for Christmas dinner. Admiral Sherman had a special motto which he affixed to all his operations orders over his signature: "Kill the bastards scientifically." It set the tone for the introduction of the two squadrons to the fast carriers of Task Forces 38 and 58.

In addition to the Marines, *Essex*'s Air Group Four (CVG-4) was composed of Navy Fighter Squadron Four (VF-4), flying F6F Hellcats, and Torpedo Squadron Four (VT-4), flying TBM Avengers. CVG-4's bombing squadron, VB-4, had been detached to make room for increased fighter strength for defense against the kamikaze threat. The air group's strength was thus thirty-six F4Us, thirty-six F6Fs, and fifteen TBMs, plus a few "cats and dogs"—specialty aircraft such as night fighters and photoreconnaissance planes—from time to time. With the fighters doing an increased amount of bombing and strafing in this phase of the war, it was still a potent striking force.

The "bedding down" period for the Corsair Marines aboard ship was in no way a leisurely process. *Essex* sortied from Ulithi before the end of the month as part of Task Force (TF) 38. The force consisted of thirty aircraft carriers and almost eight hundred other ships, either participating in or supporting landings at Lingayen Gulf in the Philippines led by Gen. Douglas MacArthur. As the saying went at the time, "With the help of God and a few Marines, MacArthur returned to the Philippines."

Probably the most frequent reaction from those who experienced the task force's departure from the vast lagoon of Ulithi was one of complete awe. It was a clear day, and on forming up and exiting the lagoon, the massive strength of the force became increasingly evident. As Colonel Millington put it, the sight of those ships from horizon to horizon "made one proud of the great strength of the U.S. Fleet and to be a part of it." The feeling was emphasized by the beautiful, "CAVU" (ceiling and visibility unlimited) day, but unfortunately that was the last day of clear weather until the month-long operation was completed.

The TF-38 mission was to enter the South China Sea and conduct a rapid series of strikes against targets in Okinawa, Formosa, Luzon, the China coast, and French Indochina. It was the first time U.S. surface ships had been in these waters off the coast of Asia proper since Pearl Harbor, and it was clearly indicative of the great gains made throughout 1944 by the U.S. and allied forces in the Pacific. However, it was not by any means a cakewalk. The South China Sea, where the Third Fleet remained for almost two weeks in a 3,800-mile circuit, was literally surrounded by camouflaged kamikaze operating bases.

The operation was a daring and deep penetration of enemy territory during which much was accomplished, but not without great cost. Plagued by foul weather, the predicted operational losses for the *Essex* Marines exceeded anticipated levels. The first of these were two pilots, 1st Lt. Thomas J. Campion and 2d Lt. Barney W. Bennett, and three Corsairs, lost in the last two days of December during operations associated with the task force movement toward the Asian coast.

The first strike mission for the Marines was launched on 3 January 1945, when Colonel Millington led a flight of Corsairs to escort VT-4 TBMs to Okinawa. On this mission two Japanese fighters attempted to intercept the bombers. Millington and his wingman turned toward them, and Millington got "score one" for the *Essex* Corsairs as he shot down the first attacking "Nick," a twin-engine fighter.

The Marine squadrons participated in a total of three strikes that day against shipping and airfield targets in southern Formosa. The total day's "bag" for the task force as a whole was 27 aircraft destroyed in the air and 204 claimed on the ground. On the minus side of the ledger for the *Essex* Marines, 1st Lt. Robert W. Mullins failed to return to the ship and was not heard from again.

On 4 January, the continued bad weather claimed yet another Marine. First Lt. Donald R. Anderson was last reported climbing through the overcast above the destroyer picket line

The horizon-to-horizon view of the Third Fleet—a tremendous
armada—just prior to the sortie from Ulithi for the South China Sea
and points north, late December 1944.

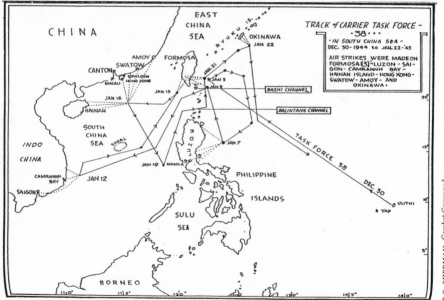

The month-long track of Task Force 38, from 30 December 1944 to
22 January 1945, which included strikes on Formosa, the Philippines,
Indochina, Hainan, Hong Kong, Swatow, Amoy, and Okinawa.

Marine pilots of *Essex* are briefed in the carrier's ready room prior to a mission against enemy installations on Formosa in January 1945.

but did not return to the ship. The day's operations were a repeat of the previous day, with two strikes to Formosa and one to Okinawa.

Zero-zero weather (clouds down to the surface and no visibility) with very few breaks stayed with *Essex* almost constantly as the attacks shifted to the northern Philippines on the sixth and seventh. Under these instrument flight conditions, the operational toll mounted to severe levels. First Lt. Robert M. Dorsett, 1st Lt. Daniel K. Mortag, and 2d Lt. Mike Kochut, all of VMF-213, entered foul weather over Appari in northern Luzon and did not return from the mission.

Of the thirteen Corsairs lost in the first nine days of operations at sea, five were lost under instrument flight conditions. In the same time period on much the same missions under the same weather conditions, the VF-4 F6Fs had no operational losses. It was a hard beginning for the hurried Marine aviation return to carrier operations.

After the strikes on northern Luzon, the force moved northwest and entered the South China Sea between Formosa and Luzon. This strong U.S. Navy fleet would be operating in the Greater East Asia Co-Prosperity Sphere (as the Japanese liked to term the overall area) for the next twelve days. It had to be a shock to the enemy high command who had since 1942 considered these waters to be another Inland Sea.

The attacks began on 11 January with another raid on the shipping and airfields in the southern part of Formosa. The fleet then continued into the South China Sea and the carriers proceeded south to launch a series of heavy attacks on enemy installations on the southeast coast of French Indochina. Cam Ranh Bay did not yield the hoped-for targets of the remains of the Japanese Imperial Navy, but the significant losses inflicted on the enemy logistic shipping present made for some notable effects. A signal was clearly transmitted to the imperial strategists that the lucrative returns from earlier conquests of southeast Asia would no longer be forthcoming.

Of the almost 1,500 sorties flown on 12 January from the three carrier task groups of the force, 984 were expended on sweep-and-strike missions covering the Indochinese coast from Tourane to Saigon. The balance—some 480 sorties —were assigned to combat air patrol missions in various areas along the objectives path from Tourane (now Da Nang) southward.

The *Essex* Marines were on CAP assignments in the morning and escorted the TBMs on the big strike against Saigon in the afternoon. They hit fields that were to become very familiar to a following generation of Marine pilots—names like Trang Bang, Bien Hoa, and Than Son Nhut. In these attacks they claimed a day's bag of twelve planes destroyed on the ground. In the shipping strikes, Maj. Fay F. Domke of VMF-213 was credited with a direct hit on a cargo ship, sending it to the bottom of the Saigon River. All told, the TF-38 score for the day was forty-seven ships totalling 157,285 tons, one of the largest shipping bags of the entire war. Enemy air opposition was generally conspicuous by its absence during the day's operations. The attacks accounted for fifteen kills in the air and almost one hundred enemy aircraft destroyed on the ground. It was indeed a big day.

On the cost side of the ledger, Task Force 38 lost sixteen planes, all to antiaircraft (AA) fire. One of these was the Corsair of 2d Lt. Joseph O. Lynch of VMF-213, who was hit and forced down very close to Than Son Nhut. Fortunately, he was rescued by friendly Frenchmen.

Lynch was still in the safekeeping of a detachment of Foreign Legion troops when the Japanese declared war on the French in March. By then, he was with a group that consisted of five Navy pilots and an Army B-24 pilot, in addition to himself. Half the Legionnaires were killed in sharp exchanges with the enemy, but the party finally made it to Din Ben. There a U.S. Army intelligence officer from Kunming, China, received them and they were flown back to Kunming in a C-47. All the downed pilots were finally returned to the United States, having survived their two-month ordeal.

Quite a few pilots of other aircraft shot down also found helpful friends who guided them to eventual freedom, but regrettably not all were that lucky. Navy Lt. (jg) Donald A. Henry of VT-4 of *Essex* was shot down in his TBM. He lost his radioman, ARM2c Ellsworth Shirley, in the crash, but escaped injury himself. He evaded capture for several weeks until he joined up with another group of six Americans, survivors of a PBM crew that had been shot down near Quang Ngai, French Indochina. The seven became the victims of a Japanese atrocity when they were eventually caught after a long chase in the mountains north of Saigon. One of their number was killed in the closing firefight; overwhelmed by superior forces, the other six offered to surrender as prisoners of war. The Japanese officer accepted their surrender and then, according to natives in the area, tied the six up and shot them one by one, kicking their bodies into a hastily dug shallow grave. It was another flagrant violation of the Geneva Convention, which Japan had agreed to observe.

One other event of 12 January was indicative of the poor intertheater communications that sometimes led to tragedy in the years of World War II. Capt. Edward P. Hartsock of VMF-124 was leading a flight of three Corsairs on CAP when a four-engine plane was spotted late in the afternoon. The plane was above an overcast in patchy cloud cover and poor visibility. When the flight approached, they received heavy fire from the larger plane's waist guns. The plane had no markings whatsoever, but Captain Hartsock withheld fire and went through the entire litany of friendly signals without any response. As the plane was apparently heading for the overcast, Hartsock decided to attack before it disappeared, since he had been briefed that the Japanese had been flying American aircraft in the area. Overhead passes were made first with some apparent hits. This was followed by a high-side run, which knocked out the port inboard engine and blew up the aircraft, remains of which fell into the overcast.

Details of the engagement were reported upon return to *Essex* and before long the plane was determined to be a B-24 from the Fourteenth Air Force operating in China. Several other B-24s had been sighted during the day's operations in Indochina, but all had had conventional U.S. markings. It was an unfortunate occurrence, but as one pilot put it, "There are ten lives in a B-24, but if it is flown by Japs it can cause a thousand deaths aboard ship." All hands were upset over the tragedy, but such outcomes regrettably do occur when communications break down or identification procedures are not observed. The *Essex* pilots were not held at fault, as Captain Hartsock had carried out every required friendly signaling procedure. Postmission analysis of Hartsock's gun camera film also clearly showed the downed B-24 to be unmarked.

Of all the strike days while the Third Fleet was making its way around the South China Sea, the attacks against Saigon and the French Indochina coast on 12 January were the tops in terms of enemy ships and aircraft destroyed. As Adm. William F. "Bull" Halsey, commander of Third Fleet, later said, it was a "strongly worded notice that control of the South China Sea had changed hands."

Task Force 38 headed north for refueling operations beginning on 13 January. Admiral Halsey kept a "flank guard's eye" out for any attempt by the remnant of the Japanese navy to interfere with the landings in Lingayen Gulf, but he also faced some other immediate problems. First, he had to determine just how to depart from the South China Sea in time to meet strategic commitments for support of the Iwo Jima operation coming in mid-February. Of even greater concern was the gathering weather, influenced by a typhoon holding sway over a large area to the south. Effects of this storm were already causing rising sea conditions in the area through which the force was moving north. The increased swells and wind strengths made it very difficult for the large ships to carry out refueling operations, and for some of the smaller ships, made refueling impossible. It was one of those complicating factors that sometimes cause decision-making to be more difficult than usual.

A fast movement to the north on the thirteenth and fourteenth helped somewhat in avoiding the worst of the typhoon's effects, permitting refueling of the carrier task groups on 14 January. This allowed them to proceed further north to launch strikes against Formosa and the coast of China on the fifteenth. The force took up position in the Bashi Channel on 15 January and made strikes against southern Formosa, with the aircraft being recovered to the west in the vicinity of Pratas Island. Moving farther west that night, strikes were scheduled for the sixteenth against a wide area of the Chinese coast from Hainan through Hong Kong and up to Swatow, Amoy, and the Pescadores.

On the 15 January strike on Formosa, Capt. Howard J. "Mickey" Finn of VMF-124 reported an innovation in the intense antiaircraft fire, which he said looked like the Japanese had put "technicolor editors into the AA act." While the color effects were startling and several planes were holed, no losses were sustained in the attack.

On the same mission, 1st Lt. Casimir J. Chop of VMF-124 reported that an enemy destroyer he was bombing "seemed to blow up" in his face. He couldn't tell whether it was his bomb hit that did it or one belonging to one of the other Corsairs in the same attack. In any case, the destroyer went to the bottom of Takao Harbor.

When Lieutenant Colonel Millington returned from the mission, he was directed to report to Rear Admiral Sherman on the flag bridge. There, the admiral informed him of the sad news that Cdr. Otto Klinsman, the commander of Air Group Four, had been lost on the morning's operations. Admiral Sherman informed Millington that henceforth he would be CAG-4. It was probably the first occasion ever in which a Marine officer had been placed in command of a Navy and Marine carrier air group. Millington held the responsible post with distinction for the remainder of his time aboard *Essex*. The assignment was a solid indication that the *Essex* Marines had become "accepted" by the ship's crew after a very hurried and difficult introduction beginning only two weeks prior.

Although the strikes against Formosa on 15 January were

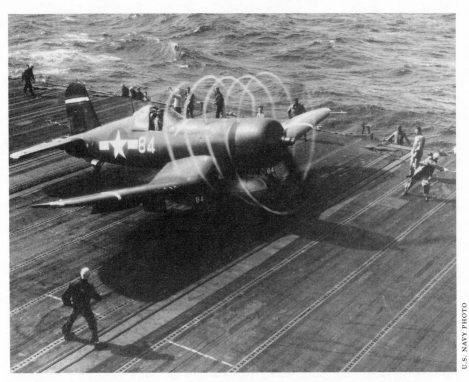

Lieutenant Colonel Millington, CAG-4, prepares for a deck launch from *Essex* in February 1945. The interesting helix often formed by the big Corsair prop is well illustrated here.

very successful, when considered with those against the Chinese coast on the sixteenth, the results of the two-day effort were not impressive. Twelve enemy ships were sunk, along with several luggers and barges, and twenty-seven ships were damaged. However, very few worthwhile ship targets were found. Although the totals for the sixteenth showed twenty-six Japanese aircraft destroyed in the air and twenty-one on the ground, the American force lost thirty planes in combat and thirty-one from operational hazards. It was one of the few times in which U.S. plane losses exceeded those of the enemy. Bad weather continued to be a factor, and the antiaircraft fire over Hong Kong was described as "varying from intense to unbelievable." From almost any analysis, one could only conclude that it was "a very disappointing two day operation."

The next three days, 17–19 January, were again plagued by foul weather and high seas as the force searched for conditions satisfactory for refueling. Moving south all the way to a point about 160 miles west of Manila, refueling was finally completed on the nineteenth. The force then set course for the Balintang Channel to exit the South China Sea.

On 20 January, as the force entered the Balintang Channel, many "bogies" (hostile contacts) were picked up on the radars, giving the Marines on CAP a chance to show what they could do. In the space of two hours, they shot down eight penetrating kamikazes, just over half the total of fifteen bagged for the day by Task Force 38. First Lt. William McGill of VMF-124 got three of these in less than as many minutes. Vice Adm. John S. McCain, commander of TF-38, responded with a message reading: "Three cheers for the Leathernecks!" It made the *Essex* Marines feel more like they were "really aboard" the TF-38 team. They were becoming accustomed to life aboard ship after a very rugged start.

Once through the Balintang Channel, the force turned north for a final strike on southern Formosa on 21 January and a parting schedule of strikes and reconnaissance missions to Okinawa on the twenty-second. Third Fleet then headed south for Ulithi, arriving there on 26 January for a few days of rest, recreation, and replenishment.

For the Marines it had been a monumental month. They had completed the first major sortie of the Marine aviation experience of the war aboard Fleet carriers. To be a part of one of the boldest and most brilliantly executed fleet operations of the air war against Japan was a matter of lasting pride for the Marine Corps. In meeting the criteria of the mission as specified — its urgencies of schedule and immediacies of preparation — high costs had been anticipated and accepted. Very poor weather through much of the first month's operations of VMF-124 and VMF-213 increased their operational losses beyond anticipated levels, but both units soon settled down and performed admirably during the remainder of their stay with Task Force 38.

Marine statistic totals for January showed: 658 individual sorties of which 95 percent were in combat; 1,973 hours flown; ten enemy aircraft shot down and sixteen destroyed on the ground; eight pilots and seventeen aircraft lost. Of the losses, only one pilot and two planes were lost to enemy action; the rest — seven pilots and fifteen aircraft — were lost to operational causes. The loss of five pilots and five aircraft could be directly attributed to inadequacies in instrument flight training. In his CAG-4 report for the period 3–22 January, Colonel Millington emphasized the "bitter lesson" that instrument flight training "would be far better learned in home training areas than . . . in enemy territory under combat conditions."

An estimate of the duration of the "settling down" period for an urgently laid-on mission of this type may be derived from the fact that all noncombat pilot losses occurred in the first nine days of operation. For the remainder of the month — almost three weeks of combat in very severe weather conditions — no pilots and just four additional Corsairs were lost to all causes other than enemy action. It was a definite indication that Corsair carrier indoctrination was over.

3   On to Japan

USS *Bennington* (CV 20)

COMMANDING OFFICER
Capt. James B. Sykes

CARRIER AIR GROUP 82
Cdr. George L. Heap

MARINE FIGHTER SQUADRON 112
Maj. Herman Hansen, Jr.

MARINE FIGHTER SQUADRON 123
Maj. Everett V. Alward

USS *Bunker Hill* (CV 17)

COMMANDING OFFICER
Capt. George A. Seitz

CARRIER AIR GROUP 84
Cdr. George M. Ottinger

MARINE FIGHTER SQUADRON 221
Maj. Edwin S. Roberts

MARINE FIGHTER SQUADRON 451
Maj. Henry A. Ellis, Jr.

USS *Wasp* (CV 18)

COMMANDING OFFICER
Capt. Oscar A. Weller

CARRIER AIR GROUP 81
Cdr. Frederick J. Brush

MARINE FIGHTER SQUADRON 216
Maj. George E. Dooley

MARINE FIGHTER SQUADRON 217
Maj. Jack R. Amende

At Ulithi, the force underwent a change of command. On 26 January, Third Fleet, commanded by Admiral Halsey, became the Fifth Fleet, under Adm. Raymond A. Spruance. (This was standard procedure during the Pacific campaign; the two admirals and their staffs alternated between planning ashore and commanding the fleet.) Task Force 38, under Vice Admiral McCain, became Task Force 58, commanded by Vice Adm. Marc A. Mitscher.

Refueling, general replenishment, training, and some recreation were routine in preparation for the next sortie. Anticipation was foremost in all minds, as the target areas for the next period included the home islands of Japan. For the Marines, the second part of the mission was of particular interest in that it would include supporting strikes at Iwo Jima in advance of the Marine divisions to be landed there in mid-February.

The *Essex* Marines were also delighted to find a heavy reinforcement for the February deployment and subsequent operations. Three carriers joined the Task Force at Ulithi, *Bennington, Bunker Hill,* and *Wasp,* each with an air group containing Marine Corsair squadrons, similar to that on *Essex.*

During the "rest" period at Ulithi, all the Marine squadrons busily engaged in intensive navigational training and indoctrination on all aspects of life on board combat ships. It was time well spent and returned good dividends in the coming weeks.

The recreational part of the stay at Ulithi consisted of visits to Mog Mog, one of the atoll's islets, where the fleet had set up what little recreational equipment was available. Up to fifteen thousand officers and men at a time could visit Mog Mog to, as Robert Sherrod, author of *History of Marine Corps Aviation in World War II,* put it, have "a touch of land and a swig of beer." It was a change of scenery at least and gave them "something different" to do.

On one occasion, a group of *Essex* Marine NCOs (noncommissioned officers) were returning to the ship from Mog Mog, when almost back to the mooring the motor launch engine quit. Without further word, the Marines tucked their caps in their belts, dove over the side, and swam for the gangway in a somewhat ragged formation. On arrival aboard, the officer of the deck lined up the dripping "Devildogs" on the quarterdeck and assigned each one to an ammunition-loading detail on a lighter alongside. After a day of this duty, their need for individual unscheduled recreational swimming dropped to zero.

On 10 February 1945, Task Force 58 got under way for its next operation. Shortly after forming up, the target was announced, 1,560 miles due north from Ulithi—Tokyo! The mission was to mount a series of fighter sweeps and strikes against airfields and industrial targets concentrated in the Tokyo area. Following that, TF-58 would begin operations in direct support of the assault on Iwo Jima, eight hundred miles to the south. It was a much anticipated time, finally at hand, for the Marine aviators. They had been waiting for many long months, since the Solomons, to get back in close support of their brothers on the ground.

For the Tokyo raids, Task Force 58 consisted of a total of 122 ships: 11 *Essex*-class fleet carriers and 5 light carriers, carrying a total of 1,200 aircraft; 8 battleships; 1 battle cruiser; 5 heavy cruisers; 11 light cruisers; and 81 destroyers. With eight Marine squadrons on board four of the big carriers, the 144 Corsairs made up about 16 percent of the fighter strength of the force. It was a potent force, but it had to be for successful penetration of the very heart of imperial Japan. The enemy was badly wounded at that stage of the war, but he still had a potent capability to inflict serious damage with the desperation kamikaze tactic.

The weather on 16 February, the first day of the TF-58 raid on Tokyo, was—as had become normal to the force—murky, cloudy, windy, rough, cold, and wet. It made target identification, intercept visibilities, and all aspects of mission navigation very difficult, to say the least. In spite of the marginal conditions, all scheduled missions were off at first light and continued through the day.

The first strike of the day came from *Essex* as CAG-4, Lieutenant Colonel Millington, led a strafing mission to Tenryu airfield. Soon after, Major Marshall, the VMF-213 commander, led his Corsairs in a mission to escort torpedo and photo planes of Air Group Four over targets of the Tokyo area.

From *Bennington*, Maj. Herman Hansen, Jr., commanding VMF-112, took eleven Corsairs on the first sweep over the Japanese mainland. Maj. Edwin S. Roberts, skipper of VMF-221, led a similar-sized sweep from *Bunker Hill*, the flagship of Admiral Mitscher. From *Wasp*, Maj. George E. Dooley, commanding VMF-216, led a group of VMF-216 and -217 Corsairs through very spotty weather to attack the Yokosuka and Tateyama airfields. It was a cold, nasty, busy day.

Maj. David C. Andre of VMF-112 had an early launch from *Bennington* on CAP and in the course of the mission, intercepted a Japanese "Betty" bomber about thirty miles off the coast and shot it down. Andre shared the kill with his wingman, 2d Lt. Carroll V. King.

Major Hansen's sweep strafed O Shima, Mobara, and Katori airfields, destroying twenty enemy planes on the ground. On the mission, 2d Lt. George J. Murray got out in front of his leader and knocked down a twin-engine Nick fighter. This wasn't exactly in line with tactical doctrine, but since the result was positive, Major Hansen decided not to "press charges." Second Lt. James M. Hamilton was hit in the strafing attacks and was forced to make a water landing, but luckily was fished out by USS *Blue* (DD 387).

The Japanese were obviously surprised by the attack at each of the three airfields and pandemonium was evident as troops scrambled for cover when the strafers hit. Antiaircraft artillery was active but the surprise factor made it much lighter than anticipated. At the end of the day, Major Hansen said to Capt. Percy Avant, another Solomons veteran, "Gee, I wish Joe Bauer, Bill Marontate, Nat Clifford, Bill Gise and the others we lost at Guadalcanal could have seen the Marines flying over Tokyo today. It would have done their hearts good."

Another VMF-112 mission, led by Capt. Donald C. Owen, could not penetrate the weather to get to its target in the Tokyo area. Instead, Owen led his flight after targets of opportunity. They hit the jackpot on the east coast of Nojima-Zaki peninsula, where they destroyed ten Betty bombers on the ground at Konoike airfield. During the action, 2d Lt. Robert B. Hamilton shot down a "Tojo" fighter that happened to be airborne. Following these attacks, Captain Owen proceeded to Hokoda airfield and the flight left three hangars burning there as a result of numerous rocket hits. Consider-

When Mount Fuji, above Tokyo, was visible, everyone knew they were in the heart of the target area.

Bennington participated in the Tokyo raid of February 1945. The weather was terribly cold and wet as crewmen respotted the deck for the second launch.

Bennington Marines are briefed for the Tokyo raids of February 1945 on a relief map of the target area. *Center, top to bottom:* Cantrel, Mobley (commanding officer, VMF-123), Clapp, and VMF-123's intelligence officer.

ing the weather and the fact that the enemy did not mount much airborne opposition, it wasn't a bad day for VMF-112.

On the second strike from *Bennington,* Maj. Everett V. Alward, commanding officer of VMF-123, took twelve of his Corsairs on a sweep over Hamamatsu and Mikatagahara with fighters from *Hornet* and *Wasp.* They shot up eight twin-engine aircraft on the ground and left a sizable tanker burning at the nearby docks. Five "Zekes" were sighted over Tokyo Bay and Major Alward climbed rapidly to engage. On his initial attack, he succeeded in sending one flaming into the bay, in spite of the fact he had incurred a good-sized hole in his left wing in the strafing attacks. Three others of his flight were also hit on the mission. Second Lt. Robert M. Cies joined up after the strafing, but disappeared during the climb to engage the Zekes and was not heard from again. Second Lts. Wallace R. Hathcox and Harry J. Bearlund were so badly damaged by both antiaircraft and enemy fighter fire that both had to make water landings near the rescue destroyer *Longshaw* (DD 559) on the way back to the ship. Hathcox got out of his plane, but his parachute billowed and dragged him under before *Longshaw* could reach him. Bearlund was rescued uninjured and returned to *Bennington* a day later.

The attack on Hamamatsu was made from altitude, to permit an initial high-speed approach to a steep strafing dive. This meant that all the Corsairs had their superchargers set in "high blower" during the climb. Normal procedure called for resetting to "low blower" on entry into a steep descent, but under the stress of combat, sometimes things like this were forgotten. This was the day for 1st Lt. Archie J. Clapp to have this lesson "grooved" into his memory.

As he was making his second pass over the field at two hundred feet, Clapp glanced at his manifold pressure gauge and what he saw "tied his gut in a knot"—the gauge was reading "ten inches over the red line." He slapped it into low blower immediately, and as he later recalled, "Fortunately the rugged Pratt and Whitney engine didn't start depositing its cylinder heads all over the airfield I was shooting up! One thing for sure, I never again overlooked the blower lever or any other critical control anywhere near enemy territory."

In the early afternoon Major Alward led another launch of fourteen Corsairs from VMF-123, along with fighters from *Wasp* and *Hornet,* to escort TBMs over the same targets. This time nine twin-engine planes were assessed as damaged. One twin-boomed "P-38 look-alike" fighter plane was destroyed on the ground, credited to the strafing run by Major Alward. On the return leg to the ships, the Hellcats and the Corsairs strafed a sizable picket boat and its destroyer escort. The picket craft was listed as probably sunk and the escort was smoking heavily when last seen. It was a busy day for VMF-123 with many pluses, but unfortunately with the noted minuses also on the score card.

Later on this active first day, Major Dooley was designated the strike leader of eighty planes from *Wasp, Hornet,* and *Bennington,* against Hamamatsu. Before the join-up, forty more aircraft were added, and in all, 120 fighters and TBMs proceeded to the target. The large strike did much damage and only suffered the loss of one TBM to antiaircraft fire. It was forced to ditch on the way home, but did so alongside a rescue submarine which was precisely on station, and the entire crew was picked up uninjured. On the way back to base, numerous small ships were encountered. Dooley dispatched elements of the formation to attack the enemy vessels and as a mission dividend, many were sunk or heavily damaged.

Unfortunately, there was one very poignant loss. On the way back to the ship, well south of Honshu, 2d Lt. Daniel V. Hayes was flying the first plane to join up on Major Dooley's lead division after the attack on the Hamamatsu airfield. Although apparently all right, Hayes began to fall back from the formation and 1st Lt. Raymond J. Gambon, the second section leader in Dooley's division, dropped back to check on him. There was much confusion as many planes were trying to rejoin the formation and all frequencies were jammed with talk, so it was not possible for Gambon to identify the pilot at the time. He gave hand signals to Hayes to close up and re-join the formation on two different occasions and each time Hayes responded but then lost distance again. Gambon went back a third time but could not get in position quick enough to get his attention. Hayes continued flying a shallow glide, right into the water. The plane sank immediately. It was not until the postmission debriefing that Lieutenant Gambon realized that the pilot was Hayes—his roommate on the *Wasp*. It was a painful incident for Lieutenant Gambon and a hard experience for the *Wasp* Marines.

Later, Maj. Jack R. Amende took four of his VMF-217 Corsairs on a mission back to Hamamatsu, again with fighters from *Bennington* and *Hornet*. In a strafing attack on some sixty enemy aircraft observed on the ground, the *Wasp* flight was credited with the destruction of six. During the join-up after the attack, Amende's plane was jumped by a Zeke, and he fell off into a shallow gliding turn. First Lt. Vernon H. Salisbury immediately got on the Zeke's tail and shot it down, but Major Amende was not seen again.

Eight more *Wasp* Corsairs were launched for a sweep over the Yokosuka and Tateyama airfields, but on takeoff 1st Lt. Roland V. Vaughn went into the water and was not recovered. Also on that mission, 1st Lt. Spencer B. Weills failed to get out of his plane when he was forced to make a water landing on retiring from a strafing pass.

On the sweep led by Major Roberts of VMF-221 from *Bunker Hill,* Capt. William N. Snider and 2d Lt. Donald G. MacFarlane shared in the kill of one Betty in the Tokyo area. The sweep also destroyed three planes on the ground, damaged another, and started fires in hangars with their strafing attacks on the target area airfields.

In another mission, the *Bunker Hill* Corsairs escorted bombers to the Nakajima Airframe Plant at Ota. En route to the target, they were jumped by a single Tojo. In the quick action, 2d Lt. William M. Pemble was shot down and was not recovered. VMF-451 Corsairs also attacked three small cargo ships escorted by two destroyer escorts in Sagami Wan on the

First Lt. Vernon Salisbury, VMF-217, got the enemy fighter that shot down his skipper, Maj. Jack R. Amende.

coast near Yokosuka. The AKs were damaged by numerous hits in the attack and one was left burning, but 1st Lt. Forrest P. Brown, Jr., was hit by antiaircraft fire from the escorts and landed in Sagami Wan. Brown was seen to get clear of the aircraft and rescue operations were alerted, but by the time they could get to the scene, it was too late and Brown was not heard from again. During the action, a "Jake" kill was shared by 1st Lt. James R. Anderson, Jr., and his wingman 2d Lt. Philip S. Wilmot.

For the fast carrier Marines, it was a momentous thrill to participate in the first major engagement over Japan. They were more than a little proud to be a part of the big event— very bad weather and some sad losses to be sure, but a seasoned performance nevertheless.

The morning of 17 February showed no improvement in the weather outlook; if anything, it was worse than the day before. In spite of the realization that it would be a short mission schedule, a few flights got off to let the enemy know the force was still at his front door.

Of the flights that launched on the seventeenth, eight *Bennington* Corsairs from VMF-112 had a mission back to the Tokyo airstrips. Major Hansen led them and was credited with shooting down an "Oscar" fighter attempting to intercept. *Hornet* and *Wasp* Corsairs also rocketed and bombed fifteen parked aircraft at Haramachida field and VMF-217 knocked down two more airborne at Haneda airfield near Tokyo. First Lt. James O. Seay was credited with an Oscar and 1st Lt. William T. Stratton, Jr., with a Zeke.

Major Alward led eight *Bennington* Corsairs of VMF-123 to join with twenty fighters from *Hornet* and *Wasp* in an attack on the Atsugi and Tateyama airfields near Tokyo. The fighters each carried four 5-inch rockets with instantaneous fuzes and used them against a military warehouse and a locomotive, destroying both. In the rocket and strafing attacks, Major Alward was so low that he came back with a mud-splattered windscreen. Alward shot down a Tojo over Tokyo Bay and Lieutenant Clapp knocked down a Zeke. Scores would have been higher, but rain freezing in the gun mechanisms caused jams and missed opportunities. In the same attacks, 2nd Lt. Edward H. Rohricht had his rudder shot off. He was able to climb and bail out, but no further word was heard from him.

With no change in the weather by midday, the remaining TF-58 schedules were canceled and the force departed the area for the support mission at Iwo Jima. For the two-day presence in the Tokyo area, force statistics showed aircraft plants and airfields were heavily hit, with 332 enemy aircraft shot down and 177 destroyed on the ground. Of the totals, twenty-one aircraft shot down and sixty destroyed on the ground were credited to the Marines.

D-day for the Iwo Jima operation was set for 19 February 1945. It had been planned for an earlier date, but several operational delays necessitated postponing its start. Direct support of the landing forces by the task force was limited to the four days it could spare from its primary mission against Tokyo. Marine air was assigned a key role in the support of the Iwo Jima assault, but only for the four days of TF-58 operations there—from D-day, 19 February, to D+3, 22 February. At that time, Task Force 58 had to set course back to the Tokyo area for the second great attack on the home islands, again in indirect support of the Iwo Jima operation.

The thought often arises in discussions about Marine air in World War II that Iwo Jima offered an ideal opportunity for close and responsive positioning of close air support (CAS) carriers. Iwo was one assault where close air support —Marine style—might have made a significant difference. Direct support of the landing forces ashore after Task Force 58 departed was left in the hands of the escort carrier group manned entirely by Navy CVE composite air groups with FM Wildcats and TBM Avengers. While these Navy support groups were willing and able, they did not provide the same level of effectiveness and teamwork as that designed into the Marine close air support system.

A few factors of the operation that would have favored

Marine-style CAS include: no continuous air opposition; generally open terrain (no jungle cover); a very small objective area (compared to Guadalcanal, Bougainville, the Philippines, and others); and the presence of several convenient and unambiguous terrain reference points. This situation was similar to that several years later at the Pusan perimeter in Korea, where Marine close air support from two CVEs was so effective. In February 1945, unfortunately, the Marine CVE program was still vigorously training in southern California. Since the Marine CVE program was not yet available, the Marine divisions appreciated the Navy air support. However, in view of the heavy casualties the Marines were sustaining in the battle for the island, the division and corps commands keenly felt the lack of the close integration and mutual understanding the Marine system would have provided. There are always "if onlys" in warfare, but an earlier approval of the Marine CVE program might have helped in reducing the high casualties sustained by the Marine divisions in the bitter thirty-five-day Iwo Jima battle.

Col. Vernon E. Megee was assigned as commander, Landing Force Air Support Control Unit (LFASCU) for the Iwo operation. In that capacity he would control all support aircraft once the landing force command had been moved ashore. When the force returned to Ulithi from the Tokyo raids, Colonel Megee and his staff boarded *Essex* for a conference on Iwo Jima D-day air support. Key personnel of the *Essex* air group assembled in the wardroom and Megee informed them that they had been assigned the mission of providing H-hour support for the Marine Corps landings on Iwo Jima. Together with Lieutenant Colonel Millington (CAG-4) and his squadron leaders, the pre– and post–H-hour strikes were finalized.

The plan called for a first strike from H minus forty-five minutes to H minus thirty-five along the flanks and high ground features of the landing beaches, followed by low-level strafing of the beaches from H minus five minutes to H-hour. The actual impact area of the strafing runs was to cover the area from the water's edge to two hundred yards ahead of the leading wave. When the landing force reached the beach, the impact area was to be moved five hundred yards inland to reduce defensive fire emanating from that depth. The strafing attacks were to be from south to north in fairly steep dives, with pullouts to be no lower than six hundred feet to avoid the naval gunfire also impacting in that area.

The plan then called for the *Essex* group to stand by for CAS missions as requested, to the limits of their time on station. The *Wasp, Bunker Hill,* and *Bennington* Marines were also to stand by for CAS missions as requested by the assault divisions. The Marines of all four carriers would participate in CAS strikes for the four days of direct support allotted for the landing.

As part of the preparation for the Iwo landing, the island had been bombed for seventy-two straight days prior to D-day. Most of this work was done by the Seventh Air Force, but naval gunfire and the Third and Fifth Fleet carriers shared part of the load. Unfortunately, the effectiveness of this bombardment was minimal. As Sherrod expressed it in his *History of Marine Corps Aviation in World War II,* "Nowhere else in the Pacific war did preliminary bombing and naval gunfire get such a black eye as at Iwo Jima."

The Japanese defenders remained deeply sheltered in their complex system of caves, prepared underground redoubts, and interconnecting lines of communication. They had adopted a concept for their defense of the island which called for minimum effort at the waterline. Instead, they planned to place their efforts into maximum fire concentrations, prelaid and zeroed in, for every feasible avenue of advance inland.

It was a devastating concept and it was put into play about two hours after the initial landing. For roughly twenty days, the daily advances were measured in yards in a murderous effort to subjugate the island. The Navy CVE carrier task group did the best it could to provide close air support, but in the words of Sherrod, "The men on the ground could only shake their heads and plunge forward with their rifles and flamethrowers." Admiral Sherman, the very experienced, longtime commander of fast carrier Task Group 58.3, in his excellent book *Combat Command,* takes a somewhat different view from Sherrod:

The jeep carriers which had been giving close support to the assault troops flew over 8,800 sorties between February 16 and March 11. They received high commendation for their destruction of enemy coast defense, antiaircraft and machine-gun positions, mortars, rocket launchers, tanks, pillboxes, supplies and troop concentrations.

Perhaps the actual effectiveness fell somewhere between these two divergent views. However, many Marine Corps analysts and historians adhere to the belief that there would have been a significant difference if a strong Marine CVE force had been available at Iwo Jima for close air support. The fact remains that the cost totaled well over five thousand Marine lives and many more thousands wounded. That terrible price, as previously indicated, generated analytical thought toward what might have been had a Marine carrier program for close support of landing forces been approved as recommended by Gen. Holland Smith early in 1944.

The D-day strikes—before, during, and after H-hour—totalled 765 sorties from the fast carriers and the escort carrier task group. More than six hundred aircraft delivered more than 130 tons of bombs, 2,250 rockets, 100 napalm tanks, and the strafing runs of 350 fighters, 170 torpedo bombers, and 65 dive-bombers. Nevertheless, the Japanese defensive concept proved an effective counter to this very strong aerial assault, even with a powerful naval gunfire force in augmentation.

The fact that the landing force got ashore and established a toehold at the beach at all could be attributed to the pre–D-day preparatory attacks, combined with those on D-day itself. But after H+2 hours, when the defending fire began in earnest against the advance inland from the beaches, the momentum of battle went significantly to the defensive concept. It made the price to take the island inordinately high.

Capt. James E. Swett, medal of honor recipient from Guadalcanal and executive officer of VMF-221, just before he boards *Bunker Hill* in 1945.

Left: Second Lt. Dwight N. Mayo of VMF-123 had a rugged day on 18 March 1945. Right: Capt. Herbert H. Long of VMF-451, a Guadalcanal ace and stalwart veteran of the *Bunker Hill* Marines.

Beginning with the afternoon of D-day, the fast carrier Marines participated in numerous large strikes in support of the laborious advances of the Marines ashore. A few missions were also flown augmenting the support strikes assigned to the escort carrier task group. For the four-day stay at Iwo Jima, however, very little of this effort could be considered true close air support as rendered in the Marine CAS system. All the support effort was of course in addition to the normal mission of the air groups, which was to provide thorough air cover of the whole operation from dawn to dusk.

On the afternoon of D-day, 19 February, *Bunker Hill* Marines under control of LFASCU were part of a strike at points of resistance inland from the beaches. The effort consisted mainly of strafing and napalm drops with very little feedback on effectiveness. On the next day, *Bennington* Corsairs flew two ground support missions in front of the 4th and 5th Marine Divisions, but the results were again difficult to obtain. Communication channels were chock-a-block. With friendly naval gunfire and artillery increasing with each hour, not to mention the continuing heavy enemy defensive fire, observation was difficult at best. The smoke and fires of the intensive battle below magnified the problems of assessing strike results from the air.

On 21 February, *Bunker Hill* Corsairs flew a support mission that was again hampered by observation and communication problems, intensified by deteriorating weather. *Bennington* Marines were also a part of a strike that rained bombs and rockets against an enemy position in front of the 5th Marine Division. A large strike from *Wasp,* including fighters from VMFe-216 and -217, targeted an enemy strong point just four hundred yards ahead of the 4th Marine Division on the right flank of the advancing ground troops. Observers described "great devastation" from this attack, and the commander, Support Aircraft, added a hearty "well done."

On the task force's last day at Iwo (D+3), eight more Corsairs from *Wasp* flew a support mission in the morning, but the weather closed in after that, ending what support the fast carrier Marines could bring to the rugged situation ashore. For the Marines, it wasn't as much direct support as they hoped it could be, but it made them feel that at least for four days they had been there with the "mud Marines." On the afternoon of D+3, Task Force 58 headed north for strikes at Chichi Jima and Haha Jima and a return to the Tokyo area, resuming indirect support of the Iwo Jima operation.

From the departure of the fast carriers on the evening of D+3, the escort carriers provided all direct air support missions until D+17. P-51s of the 78th Army Fighter Squadron arrived then, occupying airfields secured ashore on Iwo Jima. They flew missions in combination with the escort carriers' aircraft until the CVEs departed on the evening of D+20. The P-51s then flew all close support missions through D+23.

A Marine squadron, VMTB-242, also flew in from Tinian with the P-51s on D+17. They might have helped in close air support from time to time, but their primary mission was to furnish antisubmarine patrols night and day for the sea around the whole island. Their schedule was such that, with much of the squadron still in the rear echelon at Tinian, they could barely meet their primary mission, let alone provide additional CAS backup.

On 23 February, during the start of its trip back to the enemy home islands, Task Force 58 hit Chichi Jima, a subordinate base about 150 miles north of the Iwo Jima regional command. Chichi Jima and nearby Haha Jima had been hit by sizable fast carrier raids about six times, beginning in June 1944 and continuing in July and August. They had both been attacked sporadically by B-24s, B-25s, and B-29s during and after the operations in the Mariana Islands.

Task Force 58's strikes were effective, but unfortunately a very accurate antiaircraft battery situated on a prominent coastal point on Chichi Jima shot down 2d Lt. Warren E. Vaughn, a newly joined replacement pilot in VMF-123. Vaughn parachuted into the water and was seen swimming toward shore, but he was not heard from again. This same type of antiaircraft emplacement on Chichi Jima had earlier shot down Ens. (later President) George W. Bush and his TBM Avenger, but he had had the good fortune to be rescued by a standby seaplane.

Much later, after the war ended and the various enemy bases surrendered, a series of atrocities that occurred at Chichi Jima came to light. Several American aviators that were shot down there had been executed, in violation of the Geneva Convention governing the treatment of prisoners of war, the premises of which Japan had agreed to uphold. The postwar investigation of Japanese conduct at Chichi Jima revealed shocking evidence that the enemy leadership there had been involved in cannibalism. Twenty-one Japanese officers and men of the Chichi Jima command were tried before the War Crimes Tribunal at Guam in 1946. One lieutenant was acquitted, but the rest received varying sentences. Five senior officers were given death by hanging and two more received life imprisonment. The remainder received prison sentences of five to twenty years. All told, it was a barbarous incident that staggers the imagination. Just like the charges stemming from the holocaust in Europe, such conduct should remain a part of any historical record of the war in the Pacific.

After the attacks of the twenty-third at Chichi Jima, the force proceeded north to Honshu. Early on the morning of 25 February, strikes were launched against Japan in coordination with an attack of over two hundred B-29s from the Marianas. Much of the effort consisted of heavy strikes against the Nakajima aircraft plant at Ota, about fifty miles north of Tokyo, and a nearby aircraft assembly plant at Koisumi. Although the weather was bad again and hampered effectiveness considerably, both plants were heavily damaged. A summary report stated that a total of 158 enemy planes were destroyed, including 37 shot down attempting to intercept the strike groups. One of these was credited to 2d Lt. Claude O. Barnhill, Jr., who shot down a new "George" fighter on the mission. Five small vessels were also sunk and two large trains were wrecked.

The cost of this success was by no means insignificant: nine carrier fighters were lost. Five of the pilots were recovered. Of the four lost, the carrier Marines suffered two, including Maj. Everett Alward, the skipper of VMF-123, and 2d Lt. Vincent A. Jacobs of the same squadron. Alward was last seen being attacked by a Zeke over Tokyo Bay and Jacobs's fate was not known.

This was a particularly tough loss for VMF-123, as Alward had been an aggressive leader for his squadron and had brought it into prominence on the previous Tokyo raid. Fortunately for the squadron, he had an equally capable and experienced executive officer in Maj. Thomas E. Mobley, Jr., who succeeded to command.

Most of the missions on this return to the Tokyo area were hampered by the continuing bad weather conditions. Some target areas were clear at the right moment, while others nearby were "clobbered." Subfreezing temperatures and much rain caused frozen gun mechanisms and extreme frustration. Blowing snow made many types of targets very difficult to locate, with one exception: at many of the Japanese airfields, the runways had been cleared of snow, making the blacktop of the runways and taxiways stand out sharply as inviting targets. All told, however, frustration was the paramount characteristic generated by the weather. As one pilot put it, "There below was Tokyo. I spent three hours over the place. What have I got to show for it? Frostbite!"

The hardest frustration to absorb was the frozen gun firing mechanisms, especially when they became a factor in the relatively infrequent encounters with enemy fighters. In one example, Maj. Herbert H. "Trigger" Long of VMF-451 was leading a flight of Corsairs at 25,000 feet over Tokyo Bay when they mixed with an equal number of Zeroes. In Long's words:

Although the resultant dog-fight included the usual maneuvering, diving, zooming, turning and radio chatter, not a shot was fired by either side. . . . The long climb through heavy rain and many cloud layers had collected moisture in machine gun firing mechanisms and the freezing temperatures at that altitude turned firing circuits to solid ice.

It wasn't so disheartening all the time, however. *Essex* Marines had at least one "good go" in similar weather, for example, when Lieutenant Colonel Millington and two of his VMF-124 pilots, Captain Finn and 1st Lt. James L. Knight, each knocked down a George fighter while on an assigned strike mission.

During these multisquadron strikes, the reader should keep in mind that there were literally hundreds of carrier aircraft on assigned missions on any given day. With so much activity, nothing about flying was routine.

Some of the strike formations were large and difficult to maneuver in the low ceilings and visibility conditions described. Lieutenant Colonel Dooley, skipper of VMF-216 in *Wasp,* was in an eighty-plane formation en route to a Japanese target when the formation leader started a climb through the overcast without realizing how thick it was. The formation leader had second thoughts shortly after starting into the clouds, and instructed the major elements of the formation to proceed independently and seek targets of opportunity. Dooley was leading his twenty-plane *Wasp* flight on the left wing of the formation, and unfortunately the leader turned toward him. Dooley, already slow, was now on the inside of the turn and was left with no choice but to continue on course right *through* the twenty planes of the leader, or risk spinning his *Wasp* Corsairs into the drink. In that weather it was simply a miracle that there was not a single midair collision in the pass-through.

About this same time, VMF-221 on *Bunker Hill* received three replacement pilots. Replacements were furnished from a fleet pool and were usually flown aboard from the pool CVE in replacement aircraft as required. As executive officer of VMF-221, it was Capt. James E. Swett's job to take them up, run through a few tactics, and generally work them out a little before putting them on the mission schedule. While checking out the new replacements, Swett had some trouble keeping his wingman closed up and repeatedly gave him the "close up" signal (rapid movement of the control stick fore and aft) without much response from the drifting replacement pilot. He seemed to be bobbing around in the cockpit looking for something when all of a sudden he radioed, "Captain, you have a Jap on your tail!" With that, Swett— and every other captain within radio range—did a fast split "S" (a very rapid flip into a steep dive). It turned out to be a Japanese reconnaissance aircraft that had been hit by the high CAP and was burning as it went down. The upshot of the whole event was that Swett and his three neophytes were assigned to the medium altitude CAP for the next four hours. When they finally got back aboard *Bunker Hill*, the three replacements immediately received some intense schooling on radio procedures, taught personally by Captain Swett.

In the frigid weather that was typical during these operations, the water temperature was very low and the exposure time for a downed pilot's survival was a matter of a precious few minutes. It put rescue from a water landing under a very tight time requirement. One of the *Wasp* Corsairs returning from a strike had been hit by antiaircraft fire and could not lower its landing gear. The ship instructed him to make a water landing because it did not want to take a chance on a crash landing fouling the deck for the other returning aircraft. Capt. Arthur K. "Artie" Doyle, the skipper of the *Hornet*, part of the same task group as *Wasp*, heard the transmissions. He got on the radio, identified himself, and said the pilot with no gear was welcome to land on his ship "right now." Second Lt. Howard L. Hubbs (known in the squadron as "Little B") gratefully accepted the invitation at once and made a belly landing aboard *Hornet*. Captain (later Admiral) Doyle was a much beloved figure of naval aviation, known for his concern for the safety of any and all pilots under his command.

On one of the *Essex* missions, 2d Lt. Donald A. Carlson was heavily hit by AA and had to make a hard landing in a plowed field near the target. He keyed his microphone on the way down and transmitted the message, "Good luck to you guys; say 'Howdy' to my wife—I'll be seeing you at Mike's." Mike's was a Los Angeles pub that was one of the squadron's favorite hangouts. Carlson carried out his promise too, walking into Mike's six months later! He had been liberated from his Japanese captors, minus some teeth knocked out in frequent beatings, after having been starved and suffering from forty days in solitary confinement—yet another example of Japan's failure to live up to its agreement to observe the elements of the Geneva Convention for the treatment of prisoners of war.

Leaving the Japanese home islands, the force headed southwest, first for refueling operations and then to "drop a calling card" at Okinawa on the way back to Ulithi. The weather over Okinawa was much improved and strikes were launched early on 1 March with excellent results. There was no enemy airborne opposition, but the antiaircraft defenses were accurate as usual. The objectives were destruction of enemy shipping and airfields, and reconnaissance photo-mapping in preparation for the amphibious assault scheduled to take place a month later. One large cargo ship was sunk at Naha by a rocket attack executed by *Wasp* Corsairs, many small craft were destroyed, and a few planes were burned on the ground. All photoreconnaissance objectives were covered.

Capt. John P. Kelley of VMF-216 reported "lots of medium, heavy and light AA around the city of Naha." He led eight Corsairs in the attack on enemy shipping there. With Kelly's rockets tail-fuzed only, the ship's bottom was blown out and it sank in less than a minute. Kelley reported that on his second run, "only the flying bridge was above water with one Jap firing a 20-mm cannon at me *very angrily*."

On one of the *Bunker Hill* strikes, 1st Lt. Albert C. Simkunas was hit by antiaircraft fire and was forced to land in the water very close to Naha and only about a mile or so off the Okinawa shore. In the scramble to prepare for the imminent water landing, Simkunas locked his canopy open and unbuckled his chute, then inadvertently must have released his seat belt and shoulder straps. When the plane hit the water, he was catapulted over the propeller and into the sea, minus his life raft. Orbiting pilots dropped him another raft, which he successfully inflated and boarded, even as the Naha shore batteries attempted to find his range. Two OS2U seaplanes from *South Dakota* (BB 55), escorted by two *Essex* Corsairs, were dispatched to the scene and in short order Simkunas was back aboard *Bunker Hill*. A very happy outcome, especially for a rescue within a stone's throw of the capital of Okinawa. As Admiral Sherman, commander, Task Group 58.3, later wrote, "Control of the air was demonstrated when these planes landed . . . close to an enemy shoreline, picked up Lieutenant Simkunas and returned him to his ship in good condition the same day."

Following the Okinawa missions, the fast carrier force set course for Ulithi for another period of replenishment, rest, and recreation. Shortly after arrival, Carrier Air Group 4 was relieved by Air Group 83. VMF-124 and VMF-213 were detached from *Essex*. Both squadrons were assigned to the CVE *Long Island* for a welcome trip back to the United States. In more than two months of combat, the two squadrons had shot down twenty-three enemy aircraft and destroyed sixty-four more on the ground. All missions assigned had been commendably executed with accuracy and aggressiveness.

One particular point of these squadrons' noteworthy deployment warrants emphasis. Of the ten Marine squadrons deployed in the fast carriers, VMF-124 and VMF-213 had the shortest preparation time before reporting on board. It was on 3 December 1944 that the commander, Air Forces, Pacific, Vice Adm. George D. Murray, notified Adm. Ernest J. King, chief of naval operations/the commander in chief, U.S. Fleet (CominCh), that "the critical situation required the temporary employment of Marine VF squadrons on the fast carriers." The two squadrons reported on board *Essex* on Christmas Day at Ulithi, the task force sortied on 30 December, and the Marines were launched on their first mission the following day—a mere four weeks after the requirement was initially stated. The total cost of the hurried deployment—nine pilots and twenty-four aircraft—exceeded normal expectations, but unfortunately, it was a wartime expedient that had to be accepted.

On 13 March, the *Wasp* air group was similarly relieved and VMF-216 and VMF-217 were also transferred stateside, via Ewa. The two squadrons had been on board almost forty days, preceded by a hurried round trip from Guam to Hawaii for carrier qualification in January. To indicate the operational tempo, the *Wasp* Marines flew 316 sorties between 16 February and 1 March in intensive combat. The operations, almost without exception, were in the cold and very difficult weather conditions described earlier. The two squadrons shot down four Japanese aircraft and destroyed fifteen on the ground. They also sank one destroyer and five smaller craft on their various attack missions, and inflicted devastating damage to numerous airfield installations and industrial targets.

The cost of their relatively short operating period was five pilots and nine aircraft, although most of these losses were combat-associated with only a low percentage falling in the operational category. A direct comparison with the *Essex* Corsairs is tenuous at best, because of the variance in factors of flight experience, training time, and the general tempo of preparation before operating aboard in combat.

A cadre of the maintenance crews of both the *Essex* and *Wasp* Marine squadrons volunteered to stay on board each ship to help the Navy Corsair units that were new to the aircraft. In the *Essex,* the engineering officer, 1st Lt. Alexander Gagyi (a crew chief on the author's F3F at Brown Field, Quantico, in the late thirties) and forty-six men stayed in "kamikaze territory" until early June. Whoever said, "Never volunteer," didn't know the fiber of these Marines who voluntarily stayed on in the combat theater for three extra months!

In the *Wasp,* the response was the same, with engineering

officer Capt. William C. Lewis and twenty-eight men volunteering. In this case, however, the stay turned out to be one of short duration. The ship was hit by bombs a few days after the Marine Corsair pilots had departed. All the volunteers escaped serious injury, but *Wasp* suffered 302 casualties when a bomb penetrated the flight deck and exploded on the third deck below. The ship had to withdraw for extended repairs and the volunteers were detached and reunited with their pilots in the States. Both groups arrived home at almost the same time.

4 The Okinawa Campaign

USS *Bennington* (CV 20)

COMMANDING OFFICER
Capt. James B. Sykes

CARRIER AIR GROUP 82
Cdr. George L. Heap

MARINE FIGHTER SQUADRON 112
Maj. Herman Hansen, Jr.

MARINE FIGHTER SQUADRON 123
Maj. Thomas E. Mobley, Jr.

USS *Franklin* (CV 13)

COMMANDING OFFICER
Capt. Lesley E. Gehres

CARRIER AIR GROUP 5
Cdr. Edwin B. Parker, Jr.

MARINE FIGHTER SQUADRON 214
Maj. Stanley R. Bailey

MARINE FIGHTER SQUADRON 452
Maj. Charles P. Weiland

USS *Bunker Hill* (CV 17)

COMMANDING OFFICER
Capt. George A. Seitz

CARRIER AIR GROUP 84
Cdr. George M. Ottinger

MARINE FIGHTER SQUADRON 221
Maj. Edwin S. Roberts

MARINE FIGHTER SQUADRON 451
Maj. Henry A. Ellis, Jr.

On 14 March the preparation for the Okinawa invasion got under way with the sortie of Task Force 58 from Ulithi. As a measure of how the war was progressing, this sortie of Fifth Fleet had a change of plan from "hit and run" to "hit and stay." It would be operating in the Okinawa-Kyushu area continuously almost until the end of the war, in support of the 1 April assault landing and battle for Okinawa.

The immediate objective was to "soften" the airfields on Kyushu and the Japanese-held islands to the south toward Okinawa, as well as those installations on Okinawa itself. Additional objectives would be the airfields and air industrial activities in the southwestern part of Honshu, on Shikoku, and in Formosa. Nothing within reasonable range to act as a base for kamikaze attacks against the force was to be omitted from the continuous effort of the "fleet that came to stay."

With the relief of two Navy air groups, including their four Marine Corsair squadrons, TF-58 with its sixteen carriers now had a total of six Marine squadrons. The *Franklin* had arrived from the West Coast in time for the sortie, with VMF-214 and VMF-452 well established on board. VMF-214, Maj. Gregory "Pappy" Boyington's celebrated Corsair squadron of the Solomons campaign, was back in the fray with Maj. Stanley R. Bailey in command. Bailey was the only pilot hold-over from the old "Black Sheep," with the remainder in the reorganized outfit being almost entirely new.

VMF-452, under Maj. Charles P. Weiland, was entering combat for the first time. The squadron had been together for a year in training and was ready in all respects. Weiland himself had been in the Solomons, and in forming and training the unit, had the help of a few other experienced pilots. Like VMF-214, they too were anxious to get into combat. Unfortunately, the carrier tours of VMF-214 and VMF-452 on board *Franklin* would prove to be the shortest of all ten Marine CV squadrons.

After completion of refueling operations on 16 March, the force initiated a high-speed run for Kyushu. Japanese "snoopers" (reconnaissance planes) were out in force the next night, and night fighters from *Enterprise* (CV 6) brought down two, but some of the others obviously got their reports back to base. During the night hours of the seventeenth, both *Intrepid* (CV 11) and *Enterprise* had bombing attacks but neither suffered any significant damage.

Bennington also had two close calls from apparent kamikaze attempts during the early hours, both of which were shot down close aboard. Staff Sgt. William Fisher, Jr., the VMF-123 radio chief, was on the flight deck checking the Corsairs for the first launch. He described the experience in his personal diary:

Got up at 2:30 A.M., ate chow, went to our flight quarters stations at 4:30 A.M. We were spotted by Jap planes and were under heavy attack for two straight hours. At 5 A.M. one Jap suicide bomber came in at our ship just off the port bow, but was shot down about five hundred yards before he reached us by our own five inch guns . . . with the help of one of our large battleships on our port side. The Japs have been dropping flares which light the sky and water like the sun in mid afternoon. At 5:30 another suicide bomber came in at us on our starboard side and believe me, he just about made it. He was knocked out of the sky by our own 5-inch and 20-mm guns about 150 to 200 yards away. Boy was it close! I don't mind admitting I had to swallow my heart a couple three times. I was scared and if anyone on this ship saw it and says they weren't—he is a damn liar.

From all this activity, it was apparent that the presence of the force off Kyushu was no surprise to the enemy.

Bennington had been at general quarters almost continuously during the night, as had most of the force. VMF-112 was scheduled for the first predawn launch on 18 March, a sweep over Kanoya East airfield. There was some delay as pilots were ordered to man planes, and then ordered back below to the ready room as bogies penetrated the screen. On one of these turnarounds, 1st Lt. Junie B. Lohan and 2d Lt. George Murray had a real "eye opener." They had to stay in their planes on the flight deck just as the kamikaze Betty was coming straight for the carrier island on an obvious suicide run. Fortunately, they had the thrill of watching the ship's antiaircraft batteries knock down the kamikaze before he could reach the ship.

Major Hansen finally got his sweep off at 0545 during a lull in the kamikaze runs on the force. The flight of sixteen Corsairs proceeded to Kanoya without incident, but as they were letting down to attack the field, Capt. Donald C. Owen spotted an enemy flight moving out of the bright early morning sun about a thousand feet above. Hansen had his formation in a column of divisions and immediately pulled up to meet the enemy flight head on. The dogfight went at it hot and heavy from that point, but it was "all Marine." When it was over about thirty minutes later, nine enemy aircraft had been shot down and seven more damaged, but not a single Corsair had even been hit! The score for VMF-112 was as follows:

Maj. Herman Hansen, Jr.	$1/2$ destroyed, 1 damaged
Capt. Percy F. Avant, Jr.	1 destroyed, 2 damaged
Capt. Donald C. Owen	1 destroyed, 1 damaged
1st Lt. Junie B. Lohan	1 destroyed
1st Lt. Randolph Smith	1 damaged
2d Lt. George J. Murray	$1/2$ destroyed
2d Lt. Robert H. Cook	1 destroyed
2d Lt. James M. Hamilton	1 destroyed
2d Lt. Wendell M. Browning	1 destroyed
2d Lt. Deane E. Erickson	1 destroyed
2d Lt. Kenneth E. Huntington	1 destroyed, 2 damaged

Following the fight, the airfield was attacked as scheduled with two more aircraft destroyed on the ground, two hangars burned, and antiaircraft positions strafed. In the vicinity, two sampans were sunk and a radio station blasted. All told, it was a "dream mission."

When the VMF-112 mission landed, Major Mobley led fifteen VMF-123 Corsairs in a sweep over Kure and Hiroshima airfields. While crossing Shikoku inbound to the targets, a large flight of about thirty aircraft was spotted through a thin overcast about two to three thousand feet above. Mobley requested identification but received no reply, and since the flight was cruising in a disposition similar to their own, assumed they were from another carrier. As it passed above the VMF-123 aircraft, the unidentified flight executed an overhead attack on the formation in a very professional manner, by two-plane sections. The VMF-123 flight turned into the attacks, but on the first pass lost two planes and pilots, 1st Lt. Gordon K. Wooster and 2d Lt. Ralph A. Russell, with almost every plane hit to some degree. The squadron went into defensive "Thach weave" tactics and a thirty-minute dogfight ensued in which ten enemy aircraft were shot down with no further losses to VMF-123.

The abilities and the tactics of the enemy flight were of a caliber encountered only in very rare instances since the Solomons. Postwar information revealed that this was an assemblage of surviving Japanese pilots with combat experience, brought together for a last-ditch attempt to restore air-to-air capabilities to previous levels. The unit was called the *343d Kokutai,* and this was its first action. It was equipped entirely with the new radial-engine fighter called the "George."

The VMF-123 pilots in their debrief identified their assailants variously as Zekes, "Jacks," and Tojos, or as "new fighters," but postwar analyses indicated that they were all in fact Georges. The *343d Kokutai* was commanded by Capt. Minoru Genda, a naval flight leader of the Pearl Harbor attack. In spite of the setback of the initial surprise attack, VMF-123 fought a "hot" engagement and could be very proud of the outcome, a kill ratio of five to one.

It was interesting to go over the postwar technical revelations involved with this encounter. There were claims that the George could outperform the Corsair, but the results of this engagement do not seem to support that contention at all. VMF-123 pilots said they could turn inside a George, and they apparently could, judging from the results. Also it appears that the George designers were still laboring under some of the design misconceptions of the Zeke and other earlier Japanese combat aircraft. For example, some gains in performance appear to have been realized through weight reduction achieved by sacrificing fuel tank protection and armor plate. If true, it certainly didn't seem to pay off in the last-ditch George model any better than it did in the earlier model Zekes.

The George's two 20-mm guns mounted in each wing were a definite and demonstrated improvement, however, over the earlier Japanese fighters. All the VMF-123 Corsairs were "holed," and one pilot had to bail out of his crippled plane when he reached the picket destroyers on the way back to the ship. It was a miracle that eight of the Corsairs made it back aboard *Bennington* at all, and three of them were in such poor condition that they were immediately jettisoned upon landing. Nevertheless, one could conclude that American fighter design engineers were on the right track in continuing to include pilot protection and rugged construction as primary combat aircraft characteristics.

There was an especially notable performance of duty on this mission by Capt. William A. Cantrel. He was hit in the first enemy attack as were most of the others, but in the following several minutes he shot down two of the attackers and damaged two others. His plane was seriously damaged as the fight continued. He later reported that at one point he "heard a loud explosion and my plane seemed to halt in mid-air," but his engine was still running smoothly. Cantrel felt a numbness in his right foot where he thought he had been hit, but he "stayed with it" and rejoined the fight. A minute later he spotted a Corsair in trouble and his fire drove off an enemy fighter in the midst of a high-side run.

About the same time, and as the dogfight was breaking up, Major Mobley was hit in the cockpit by machine gun fire, and his instrument panel was shot out. Not knowing that Cantrel had been hit, Mobley turned the lead of the mission over to him for the join-up and return to the ship. Captain Cantrel took over, joined up the formation and started back to base, even though by this time he was bleeding profusely and in considerable pain. Back at *Bennington,* Cantrel let the more heavily damaged planes land first and when he landed he had very little fuel left. He was lifted from the plane and turned over to the medics who removed five pieces of shrapnel from his right foot. It was a memorable performance for which Captain Cantrel was awarded the Navy Cross.

Second Lt. Dwight N. Mayo also had a particularly rugged flight on this mission. In the encounter, he had gotten his "tail shot full of arrows before someone chased the guy off me." By then he had fallen well behind the rest of the flight, so he went to full throttle to catch up. His guns suddenly "cooked off" for some reason and he had to shut off his gun switches to stop them. Almost back to the formation, Mayo saw a George coming up from behind on the left side of the flight. He made a sharp left turn to get a shot at the attacker and at that moment all except about six inches of his right stabilizer and elevator broke off! As he later described the situation:

Have you ever been thrown into a violent inverted spin with full throttle on? Not the most fun I ever had. My straps were loose—we ordinarily flew that way, so we could move around for better visibility. The spin threw me away from the controls, and my head was banging on the canopy. I could not reach the stick, but did manage to get my hand on the throttle, pulled it back and the intensity of the spin lessened. I then got my toes around the stick, got it back to where I could grab it, and I then pulled it back. The aircraft came out of the spin easily but I had lost altitude from 14,000 down to 5,000 feet in the process. . . . We were then over the Inland Sea and after I got the aircraft under control, I was all by myself so I headed back for the Task Group.

On the way back, the whole situation got to him and he became violently ill. In attempting to keep from "messing up the cockpit," Mayo opened the canopy, but the slipstream only made it worse. In order to see out while handling the disabled plane, he had to leave the canopy open even though, wearing only a G-suit and a summer flight suit, he became thoroughly chilled. As the first plane back to the ship, Mayo took up his landing orbit overhead, but there were some delays while the ship got off a launch. In a short while the rest of his flight also returned and he joined on them. After further delays due to kamikazes in the area, it was finally his turn to land. He assessed his situation:

Landing gear? No—inoperable; flaps, the same; tail hook—long since down because it came down with loss of hydraulic pressure. I was the only plane making landing passes in the Task Group and on the third pass, I got a cut. I caught a wire about the time I hit the first barrier, and I was safely aboard. They counted forty-one 20-mm holes in the airplane before they threw it overboard.

It is completely understandable why Mayo remembered this mission in detail some fifty years later. It was a rugged day, for certain, but in this case the final outcome was a happy one.

The "box score" for this VMF-123 mission showed:

Maj. Thomas E. Mobley, Jr.	1 George destroyed, 1 damaged
Capt. William A. Cantrel	2 Georges destroyed, 2 damaged
Capt. William E. Roques	1 George destroyed
1st Lt. Harold D. Shields	1 George destroyed
2d Lt. George H. Spierring	1 George destroyed
2d Lt. Edward Milhem	1 George destroyed
2d Lt. Dwight N. Mayo	1 George damaged
2d Lt. Frank Kurchinski	1½ Georges destroyed
2d Lt. R. J. McInnis	1½ Georges destroyed

The remaining day's activities for the *Bennington* Marines consisted of a shipping strike to Kagoshima Wan, where a convoy of merchant ships had been spotted; a search mission about three hundred miles to the west toward the Chinese coast looking for the remnants of the enemy navy; and another strafing mission by VMF-123.

The strike to Kagoshima was led by Captain Owen with seven VMF-112 Corsairs. They were subjected to heavy anti-aircraft fire from the ships, the harbor defenses of Kagoshima, and Sakura Shima, but obtained direct hits on two of the ships they found moored at Sakura Shima. Second Lt. Timothy C. Clark got his hit just aft of the superstructure of one ship and 2d Lt. Deane E. Erickson dropped his 500-pounder on the bow of another. Clark was hit by AA in his run, but in spite of the damage to his plane, rejoined the formation and participated in a rocket attack on a third ship and in various strafing runs on the way out of the area. The strafing attacks were against a small shipyard, an army camp barracks, and several minor ships, which were set on fire. At the foot of the bay, the flight encountered a covey of picket boats, which were closing on a downed American pilot in his raft. Strafing passes drove them off and permitted an OS2U seaplane to land in the bay and rescue the pilot.

Just after leaving the Kagoshima Wan area, Clark's plane began to trail smoke, and with his engine failing, he prepared to make a water landing. He ditched successfully in the open sea, but could not jettison his canopy and went down with the plane. A thorough search revealed no trace, taking the edge off an otherwise very successful mission day.

Major Andre of VMF-112 led the inconclusive search for the elusive surviving enemy warships, while Maj. Donald P. Frame of VMF-123 took the last *Bennington* attack mission of the day back to Shibushi and the adjoining area. Major Frame had hydraulic problems on the way back to *Bennington* and was forced to land early on *Wasp*. As chance would have it, it would be some time before Major Frame got back to *Bennington*.

The *Bunker Hill* Marines also had a big day on 18 March over Tamitaka airfield, as VMF-221 knocked down thirteen Zekes on one mission and later in the day VMF-451 knocked off another. In the VMF-221 fight, the tally showed the following:

Capt. John B. Delancey	1 Zeke
Capt. Mitchell L. Parks	1 Zeke
Capt. William N. Snider	3 Zekes
1st Lt. Joseph Broccia, Jr.	1 Zeke
1st Lt. John McManus	1 Zeke
1st Lt. Wesley S. Todd	1 Zeke
2d Lt. Dean Caswell	3 Zekes
2d Lt. Donald G. MacFarlane	1 Zeke
2d Lt. Richard Wasley	1 Zeke

This made it without a doubt the best VMF-221 day in the deployment to date—a very satisfactory mission!

Over on the *Franklin*, 2d Lt. Ransom R. Tilton of VMF-214 had a very interesting and commendable first-ever combat mission on the eighteenth. Assigned to the first division of a combat air patrol led by Maj. Warren H. McPherson, Tilton had already started his engine when McPherson climbed up on his wing and told Tilton that he was taking Tilton's plane because he could not get his own plane's engine started. Tilton got out, but then decided to try McPherson's plane and got an immediate engine start. This caused a slight delay in his launch; the air officer, Cdr. Joseph Taylor, radioed Tilton in a "cool and understanding voice" that he would delay his launch until the engine was warmed and all was ready for takeoff.

Tilton was launched about number six or seven instead of second. As he climbed for the join-up he "cut the angle" toward the downwind leg, but was surprised to see that all the mission aircraft were joining on him. Nonplussed, he took the vectors transmitted to McPherson and the entire formation flew the CAP mission with him in the lead! The aircraft were vectored around over the force investigating several bogies, although the mission was generally uneventful. On return to the ship, Major McPherson complimented Tilton on his performance. He explained that since Tilton was doing such a fine job in the lead, he saw no reason to confuse the entire mission by trying to make a change over the very crowded radio frequency. Tilton remembered it as being like a "big league rookie hitting a grand slam on his first time ever at bat."

The eighteenth of March was literally a "furious" day of operations for Task Force 58 and its four fast carrier task groups, beginning with fighter sweeps before first light. Forty-five airfields were attacked by the force, with almost all the buildings left burning at each one. A total of 102 enemy aircraft were downed and 275 were destroyed on the ground. Marine Corsairs accounted for thirty-seven of the aerial kills: nine by VMF-112 and ten by VMF-123 of *Bennington*, four by the *Franklin* Marines, and fourteen by the Marines of *Bunker Hill*. The air group of the *Bennington* flew 186 combat sorties that day, with the Marines flying 78 of the total.

The intensive activity of 18 March, particularly the attacks on the Kyushu airfield havens of the kamikazes, was extremely beneficial in preparation for the Okinawa campaign. It was largely responsible for the absence of suicide operations against the force in the first few days of the Okinawa landing. This gave the landing Marines an opportunity to get unloaded and established ashore for almost a week after the Okinawa D-day on 1 April.

The eighteenth was not without its costs, however. *Bennington* lost one Corsair, as described earlier, and *Franklin* lost three. Of the three from *Franklin*, 2d Lt. Thomas D. Pace of VMF-452 was killed; another Marine was rescued immediately by a handy OS2U.

Second Lt. John P. Stodd of VMF-214 was the pilot of the third *Franklin* airplane that went down. He got into his life raft quickly and busily started "paddling toward China." However, as soon as his squadron mates had to leave their orbit above him, Japanese boats approached and took him into custody. He was later learned to be a prisoner of war.

Stodd's experience as a POW was one more example of brutal treatment by the Japanese and their failure to observe the Geneva Convention premises. He was eventually incarcerated at Ofuna in the Tokyo area—the same POW camp where Major Boyington, the former VMF-214 skipper, resided for much of his time in custody. Stodd missed seeing Boyington at Ofuna by only a week; the most famous of the "Black Sheep" was transferred to another camp just before Stodd arrived. Stodd almost did not survive the experience, but the war ended just in time. At his liberation, he weighed less than ninety pounds and required a lengthy hospital stay prior to his release from active duty. His sense of humor remained intact, however. He stated that if he had returned from this first mission safely, he would have "doubled his total WW II combat hours!"

The night of 18–19 March was continually busy with tracking down and warding off attacks of many Japanese penetrators. The night fighters were very busy all night, and with the shipboard AA batteries doing their part from time to time, there was little sleep for anyone. Much worse was to follow on the next day, however.

Very early on the nineteenth, one of the attackers got through and *Wasp* took a bomb hit. The bomb penetrated three decks, flamed a plane on the hangar deck, and exploded on the deck below. The multiple effects caused heavy fires on the hangar deck and totally destroyed the galley area, inflicting casualties of 101 killed and 269 wounded. Amazingly, the fires were under control in fifteen minutes and the ship was recovering planes by 0800. *Wasp* operated in the area for several days before retiring for repairs, taking along Major Frame of VMF-123, who had made an emergency landing there the previous day.

On board *Franklin*, meanwhile, the first launch was off at about 0530 and approximately two-thirds of the air group was airborne on various missions. By 0700, the second launch was about ready to go in order to clear the flight deck for recovery of the aircraft of the earlier launch, anticipated back aboard about 0745.

Thirty-one planes were on deck, engines turning up and all aircraft loaded for their assigned missions. Twelve Corsairs on deck were armed with 11.75-inch Tiny Tim rockets, the first time these potent weapons had been assigned for use against the Japanese. The remaining torpedo planes and bombers were carrying a full load of general purpose bombs and 5-inch rockets.

Just as the first aircraft were taking off, a single enemy "Judy" bomber dived out of the low cloud cover over *Franklin*. The enemy pilot dropped two medium bombs and scored two devastating direct hits on the ship. Both went through the flight deck, the first one just aft of the forward elevator and the second well aft of the island but on the deck centerline. The explosions on both the hangar deck and the flight deck shot a wall of flame and debris the length of each, leaving very few survivors, on the hangar deck particularly. The instantaneous effects were monstrous fires throughout the

View of *Franklin* from the bow looking aft, taken from *Santa Fe*.

Aircraft wreckage on the flight deck of *Franklin* after fires were extinguished and the ship had regained power, cast off the tow, and headed south at 18 knots.

Second Lt. Kenneth E. Huntington of VMF-112, the lone Corsair in the initial attack on *Yamato*. He was credited with a bomb hit on the forward turret of the big battleship, which silenced its guns.

Maj. Herman Hansen, Jr. (shown here after his promotion to colonel), who became an ace while leading VMF-112 on his twenty-fifth birthday. He got three of the suiciders and the Navy Cross on 12 April, an unsurpassed birthday present.

ship, with a billowing cloud of smoke and flame enveloping the whole vessel as she turned out of the wind and went dead in the water.

Almost immediately, all power was lost and compartments throughout the ship went dark, extending the massive confusion confronting the fire and rescue efforts on all sides. The fire-fighting was effective at first on the forward portions of the flight deck, but this was soon inhibited as the aircraft fires on both decks began to detonate the loaded ordnance. The ship was wracked with major explosions, which threw debris out hundreds of yards from the ship. Especially terrifying were the Tiny Tim rockets with their massive warheads. These cooked off and shot out of their burning aircraft mounts, coursing the length of the flight deck and beyond, with the huge orange flame of the rocket motors spiralling after.

These chaotic conditions went on for four hours while other ships did what they could to help the stricken carrier. Many of the survivors were blown off the ship and many were forced to jump as a last resort in escaping the flames and continuing explosions. The cruiser *Santa Fe* (CL 60) came alongside at about 1050 as the explosions subsided somewhat, and Capt. Lesley E. Gehres, skipper of *Franklin,* ordered all the wounded and all the air group personnel transferred to her. *Santa Fe,* with her engines holding her against the exploding carrier, took on board 826 men in thirty minutes and remained alongside for three hours rendering assistance of all kinds.

About one hundred officers and six hundred men remained aboard to continue fighting fires, and to form rescue parties as additional parts of the ship were penetrated. The cruiser *Pittsburgh* (CA 72) got a towline over to *Franklin* as progress was made against the fires, and *Santa Fe* pulled away. *Pittsburgh* was able to swing the carrier toward a southerly heading and, making about 6 knots, set course away from Japan, by then only about forty-five miles distant.

In her crippled condition, *Franklin* was a tempting target

so close to the enemy coast. The Japanese made numerous attempts to finish off the gallant ship, but the CAP and the task group antiaircraft fire were successful in warding off each try.

As *Franklin* made more progress aboard with the fires and damage control, she was able to get up speed to about 18 knots and the towline was dropped. She proceeded toward Ulithi, escorted by the two cruisers and several destroyers. On the way, many of the wounded were transferred to other ships for the direct run to hospitals at Guam.

The damage absorbed by the ship had no parallel in the entire Pacific war. With a very short stop at Ulithi and another at Pearl Harbor, she continued on to New York to enter the Brooklyn Navy Yard for major repair work. The end of the war in August overtook the repair effort, however, and she did not return to combat.

Franklin lost 724 dead and 265 wounded. Among the Marines of Franklin's two Corsair squadrons, sixty-five were included in that number: six officers and twenty-six men of VMF-214, and one officer and thirty-two men of VMF-452. It was a lamentable two-day combat tour for both squadrons. But ship and crew gave a lasting example of what determined leadership can accomplish in a modern version of "don't give up the ship."

There was a lot of work and hope expended for such a meager return. Lieutenant Tilton of VMF-214 expressed the feelings of both squadrons fifty years later:

Our big regret and disappointment was that we had trained hard for over two years, thought we were capable and only lasted two days in combat.

Seemed to me that if Capt. Lesley Gehres had had the ship at General Quarters in lieu of Condition 3-Easy, someone might have shot that Jap plane down before he hit us.

Tilton may well have been right in his view. However, it is only fair to point out that the ship had been at general quarters most of the night, and some relaxation of the crew could well have been in order. All hands had to have some breakfast, for example. Within condition 3-Easy, this could be done in relays as long as the ship's integrity was maintained below the waterline. The comment nevertheless shows the depths of the disappointment both units still felt five decades later.

In the tragedy of this remarkable *"Franklin* saga," there were hosts of heroes, some known, some unknown; some among the survivors, others hidden forever within the tragic casualty statistics. Many members of the crew were awarded citations in the following months for their conspicuous gallantry, ranging from the two Medals of Honor down through the awards hierarchy. These have been well documented elsewhere and may be seen in detail in historical coverage of all aspects of the *Franklin* disaster.

The *Franklin* Marines compiled many harrowing experiences in surviving the holocaust of 19 March, some of which are described below. There were three separate groups of survivors: pilots who were airborne at the time the ship was hit, those who were blown overboard by explosion or were forced to abandon ship by jumping into the water when trapped by the tremendous fires, and those who remained on board through the crisis, many seriously injured, waiting until they could safely be transferred to another ship for evacuation to hospitals.

First Lt. Kenneth E. Linder had been assigned as the second section leader in the four-plane division of *Franklin*'s CAG, Cdr. Edwin B. Parker, Jr. When the launch started engines, Linder's plane was slow to warm up and the flight deck officer shunted him out of line until he was ready to go. As a result, he was launched about sixth instead of in his normal number three spot. His was the last plane off the deck before the carrier was hit.

As he climbed to the join-up, he cut the angle on the planes ahead of him to move into his proper position. Passing through a thousand feet, he was "astounded to see a plane with the red meat balls on the wings." He closed on it and opened fire, seeing his tracers hitting the enemy plane.

In a matter of seconds, he was close enough to see the tail-gunner slumped over and not firing. The Judy pulled up sharply into the cloud cover with Linder close behind. When he realized the enemy pilot was planning to try to complete a loop, Linder rolled out because he did not have enough altitude to follow. As he did, he watched the Judy go straight into the ocean. It was only after they returned from the mission that they realized this was the Judy that had bombed *Franklin*. Final analyses showed that Commander Parker had also fired at the Judy moments before, and thus credit for the kill was shared between Parker and Linder. The latter also laid claim to the sad distinction of being the last Black Sheep to shoot down an enemy aircraft in World War II.

The pilots who were airborne when the bombs hit landed on several other carriers. If there was no tie-down or storage space available on the carrier, the Corsairs were unceremoniously jettisoned over the side as soon as the pilot vacated the plane. On carriers where space was available for their aircraft, the Marine pilots flew missions for several days with the host ship's air group. In some cases, it was a lengthy time before the Marines got back to their own squadrons—some not until arrival back in the States. The pilots came aboard in their mission clothing, of course, and many had no way of replacing what they had on. Most of the pilots had no opportunity to get back to the *Franklin* for possible salvage of any personal gear left on board prior to their mission launch. Second Lt. Kenneth G. Fiegener of VMF-214 spent over a month in his mission flight suit until he got back to the naval air station at Miramar near San Diego, where he could get new uniforms and other clothing.

Capt. Warner O. Chapman, a Guadalcanal combat veteran and assistant flight officer of VMF-214, was among a group of pilots who were in the ready room at the time the ship was hit. One of the bombs detonated directly beneath the ready room. Captain Chapman later described the gripping story of what these survivors endured.

Virtually everyone standing had shattered ankles or legs from the concussion. I was seated but gained a broken ankle from shrapnel coming through the deck and my left arm was broken in two places as the arm of the chair accelerated upward faster than my arm. The deck was split and the inferno below visible. I must have been momentarily knocked out because there is an obvious time lapse between sensing the explosion and being under the debris from the overhead, and crawling out in darkness to the catwalk outside. We must have individually worked our way out and gone over the side when we found we were trapped by flames around us with no way to work forward. . . . I saw no one there when I emerged although periodically someone would appear and shortly go over the side.

Chapman went on to relate that after he had been in the cold water for about an hour, the plane guard destroyer picked him up, along with more than two hundred other survivors. The destroyer had a cargo net over the side but with his injuries and the immersion effects, Chapman could not climb up the net. A sailor jumped in, picked him up "like a sack of potatoes," and got him up the net and aboard. His arm was then splinted up, and the next day, he was transferred by highline to the cruiser *Alaska* (CB 1), which had an orthopedic surgeon assigned.

Chapman and about eleven others eventually made it back to the States together, via two more ships and the hospital at Guam. The trip to Guam included two more highline transfers, one in heavy weather. The "breeches buoy" or highline transfers get exceedingly interesting in heavy weather as the two ships roll with the sea. The ships are fairly close together, but as they roll, the lines tend to go from normal to completely slack (and wet), and then snap back to completely taut. For a wounded "passenger," it can be a painful transit on occasion, but it is the only practical way one can be passed from ship to ship in many situations.

Off Okinawa, while still in *Alaska*, Chapman and his squadron mates, including 2d Lts. Carroll K. Faught and William H. Dancy, Jr., got to "participate" in the prelanding bombardment of that island. The medics had insulated them, however, against the shock and noise of the firing as the heavy battle cruiser carried out its mission, so they saw little of the action. Altogether, it made for a rather long, drawn-out trip to the hospital for Chapman's survivor group. Faught unfortunately had to have a leg amputated on board the *Alaska*, and Dancy had very painfully shattered ankles, injuries which lengthened his stay at the hospital at Guam.

Second Lts. Arthur O. Schmagel, Albert A. Sibbernsen, and Ransom R. Tilton of VMF-214 were not on *Franklin*'s flight schedule until later in the day on 19 March. They were observing the launches from the catwalk when the Judy's bombs hit the ship, and they were blown into the sea by the initial explosions. All three suffered flash burns from the enveloping wall of flame as the two bombs penetrated and exploded. In the water Tilton had trouble staying afloat because his life preserver was getting saturated. He saw Tech. Sgt. Irwin R. Schwartz swimming toward him without any flotation gear, and the thought crossed his mind that Schwartz would want to hang on to him. With the already-precarious condition of his life preserver, he was afraid that both would sink. However, when Schwartz swam up, he said, "Lieutenant, there's a destroyer over there, so let me pull you over to it." A chagrined Tilton told Schwartz that if he could swim over to the destroyer, he should do it alone, unencumbered, and ask them to send someone back for him. Schwartz promptly did so and both were soon safely aboard.

Tilton, Schwartz, Schmagel, and Fiegener were all eventually picked up by the *Hickox* (DD 673), and subsequently transferred to appropriate medical echelons. An interesting follow-up occurred some twenty-four years later, when now-Colonels Schmagel and Fiegener, then on duty at Headquarters Marine Corps, were invited to be present at the Brooklyn Navy Yard for the decommissioning of *Franklin* from the reserve fleet. They attended the ceremony and while on board the ship, Colonel Fiegener's attention was invited to the ship's log. There, among the missing in action, was listed 2d Lt. Kenneth E. Fiegener of VMF-214.

At 0400 on that fateful day, Major Weiland, skipper of VMF-452, was in the ready room preparing for a fighter sweep scheduled for launch at 0500. The sweep had the mission of attacking targets near Kobe, Osaka, and Nagoya, with particular attention to the Kawanishi aircraft engine plant west of Osaka. The mission launched on schedule and proceeded as planned. As Weiland reported later, "It seemed as if every plane in the United States Navy was flying that day."

After some early low hanging cloud layers, the sun took hold and it turned into a CAVU day over Shikoku and Honshu. On returning to the force about 0900, the flight identified itself as friendly with the prescribed signals. As they passed the destroyer screen, they observed a cloud of smoke on the horizon. It was soon identified as being their "home," the *Franklin*.

Weiland's group was instructed to land aboard the *John Hancock* (CV 19), but after doing so, space became a problem, as *Hancock* had a strike group aloft and it was due to return very soon. The decision was reached for Weiland's ten Corsairs to take off again—five to land on *Intrepid* (CV 11) and five on *Yorktown* (CV 5), all in the same task group.

First Lt. Peter L. Schaefer had been in the VMF-452 ready room early on the nineteenth to be briefed for a later mission. When the briefing was over, he exited to the catwalk to watch the strike group take off. Just as he arrived, Schaefer noticed a twin-engine plane swoop by and wondered what "that damn fool was doing right in the middle of a launch?" Then he saw the two bombs being released and penetrating the flight deck just a few feet from where he was standing. The flash fire that followed melted the synthetic material of his flight suit and burned his face, making him decide immediately that the best thing he could do was to go over the side. Schaefer did not follow the prescribed method of jumping into water from such a height feet-first, but in his hurry, went head-first instead. Fortunately he hit the water right and was not further injured. He kicked off his "boondockers" to swim better, knowing that he had to swim fast outward from the propellers. He could plainly hear and feel vibrations from the props as the ship entered a hard turn. Schaefer was in the water for about two hours before he too became a passenger in destroyer *Hickox*. Once aboard, the medics peeled the burned skin from his face and applied sulfa and vaseline-soaked gauze. Schaefer made a miraculous recovery.

Also in the ready room with Schaefer had been 1st Lts. Wallace Mattsfield, James F. Ormond, and Joseph E. Warren. The first explosions knocked them down, extinguished the lights, and rapidly filled the compartment with smoke. Ormond was unable to walk on his left foot, and Mattsfield could not get up at all. Mattsfield was later found dead in the ready room; he had apparently been knocked unconscious and succumbed to smoke inhalation.

Although both were dazed, Ormond, hopping or crawling, and Warren, tried all exits but found nothing except intense flames at each. They went back to the flight deck door a second time, and this time the flames had subsided briefly. Ormond was able to crawl across the flight deck to the gun turret forward of the island. There he met up with 2d Lt. John W. Rogalski and the two helped each other as best they could. Warren found his way out of the ready room onto the flight deck catwalk where "there were explosions going on all around me." Having no other choice, he went over the side with neither Mae West nor life preserver. He landed right beside a naval officer who had flotation, and the two clung together until rescued by the destroyer *Marshall* (DD 676).

First Lt. Baxter R. Little, scheduled for a mission later in the day, had returned to his bunkroom forward in the ship when the bombs hit. When VMF-452 had come aboard, they had been told, "When off duty and in the event of an emergency, assemble in the Wardroom." Little remembered these instructions and carried them out at once. However, there he found himself trapped with many others, including 2d Lt. Fred E. Olson, a former policeman and the squadron's intelligence officer. All hatches in the wardroom were "dogged" down, there were no lights, and the compartment was filling with smoke. As the tendency toward panic began to grow, Olson grabbed him and told him to wet his handkerchief in the water pitcher on the table and get under the table with him. Holding wet handkerchiefs over their noses and staying still made breathing much easier and calmed them down until rescue occurred after what seemed a very long time.

Beginning early on the nineteenth, despite the damage to *Wasp* and *Franklin,* sweeps and strike groups were launched to attack shipping discovered by photoreconnaissance the previous day. The enemy ships were concentrated at the major naval bases at Kure and Kobe on the Inland Sea. This was the first time these Inland Sea targets had come under attack. Finding the ships was of special interest because they were the prime targets Admiral Halsey had hoped to find in the South China Sea a month or more earlier. All the airfields in the southwest Honshu area were also hit heavily during the day.

For the Kure shipping strikes, the *Bunker Hill* air group was joined by strike groups of other carriers of the force, with the *Bunker Hill* CAG designated as the attack director. As the flight approached the Kure base, the CAG directed that half the bombers should attack ships in the harbor. As he drew closer to the base and could see what ships were actually there, however, he quickly changed that to put all the bombers on the ships. The concentration of warships in the harbor was such that it really constituted the remains of the Japanese navy. There were three carriers, one battleship, and several cruisers, destroyers, and auxiliaries in the base harbor! Antiaircraft fire was extremely intense and integrated and may have been effective enough to lessen the damage sustained by the ships somewhat. In spite of this, many of the ships were hit with damaging effect. The battleship and all the carriers were hit at least once as were the cruisers. The *Bunker Hill* group concentrated on the carriers, putting a large hole in the side of *Katsuragi* on a skip-bombing run and knocking an elevator out on its sister ship, *Amagi*. Three devastating hits were made on *Ryuho,* one putting a huge hole in her flight deck and another blowing her number three elevator completely out of the well. "Trigger" Long of VMF-451 made his presence felt with rocket hits in the structure of the hangar deck and in the bulkhead of the entrance to the engineering spaces below decks. After this day's treatment, *Ryuho* never put to sea again.

It was a "find" to locate these prime targets in harbor all right, but it had its costs. The *Bunker Hill* air group lost two SB2Cs in the attacks on the shipping, plus a badly shot-up bomber and its gunner when it crashed off the bow attempting to get back aboard. Fortunately the pilot was rescued by a plane guard destroyer. Also, on the mission 2d Lt. James G. Turner of VMF-451 was last seen when he exploded a close aboard Zeke and flew into the debris. He did not return from the mission.

To add to the day's shipping bag, Task Force 58 counted 97 enemy aircraft shot down and 225 more destroyed on the ground. It helped take some of the sting out of what happened while the mission was in progress, namely the *Franklin* disaster and the hit on *Wasp*. For the Marines involved, it also took on the aspects of a partial "pay back" for the associated losses within VMF-214 and VMF-452.

VMF-112 of *Bennington* was also busy early on 19 March. Major Hansen led sixteen of his Corsairs in a sweep over Kanoya East airfield. They were intercepted by twenty Zekes as they arrived over the field at 19,000 feet. In a short fight, the Corsairs shot down nine of the interceptors without a loss. After the enemy fighters broke off this very successful encounter, the sweep continued with the attack on the Kanoya East airfield. Flak was present in quantity, as always, but the Marines destroyed or heavily damaged buildings, hangars, and line installations. All aircraft returned to the ship without further incident.

For the next few days, some of the "visitors" from *Franklin* flew missions with the host air groups, but in a short while, steps were set in motion to reunite each refugee faction with its parent unit. As a typical example, Major Weiland's group from VMF-452 went via highline to *Hazelwood* (DD 531) for a very rough two-day trip, followed by another heavy weather highline to *Bougainville* (CVE 100) en route to Guam. *Bougainville,* an operating carrier, had taken so many refugees aboard, she seemed more like a troop transport for the run to Guam, arriving there 29 March. It was a very rough ten days for all the survivors, but each was thankful to have made the trip.

With *Franklin* out of the war, the carrier Marines were reduced to four squadrons, two each in *Bunker Hill* and *Bennington*. On 20 March, *Bunker Hill* was part of the group escorting *Franklin* and other heavily damaged ships to the south away from the Japanese coastal areas. Its air group flew CAP over the damaged ships, which also included *Hornet, Intrepid,* and *Enterprise*. *Franklin,* for the first two days of the movement of the damaged element of the force, was still being towed slowly by *Pittsburgh*. Although the kamikaze tactic was a desperation move and ultimately a losing strategy, its effectiveness was clearly evident on this occasion. It should be noted though that all but *Franklin* returned to combat after a brief repair period.

By the twenty-second, *Franklin* was under her own power and the crippled ships were out of the most dangerous area. The carrier task groups replenished and refueled, in preparation for the renewal of strikes on Okinawa scheduled for 23 March.

The flak in the Okinawa area continued to be intensive, accurate, and tough, and seemed to get more so each day. On 24 March, 2d Lt. Richard Wasley of VMF-221 was hit in a bombing run and had to bail out. Unfortunately he was either struck by the plane when he jumped or was wounded when the plane was hit, and his chute was never seen to function. On the same day, Maj. Emerson H. Dedrick of VMF-451 brought his badly damaged Corsair back to the ship, but had to ditch while on the downwind leg of his approach. He was lost in the crash and no wreckage was recovered. It was a bad day not only for the *Bunker Hill* Marines but also for the air group as a whole; the CAG, Cdr. George M. Ottinger, was hit by AA and went down offshore. He was not seen again.

The daily attacks in the Okinawa area by the fast carrier task groups continued through the landing on L-day, 1 April. *Bunker Hill* sent a strike to Minami Tori Shima, about 150 miles east of the island, on 28 March. For a welcome change, it was a CAVU day, but the airfield's antiaircraft defenses were unchanged—intense, of all calibers, and very accurate. Capt. John L. Morgan, Jr., of VMF-451 was shot down over the target and was not heard from again. The Navy squadron also had an aircraft hit in the attacks on the field, but the pilot successfully ditched near the picket line and was rescued.

On the next day, the Navy elements of the air group had a two-division collision as the planes emerged from climbing through a 5,000-foot overcast. The operational toll was five aircraft and eight crewmen—a tragic price that shows the tremendous risks instrument operations posed during World War II that today's technologies make commonplace.

On L-day, Marines from both *Bunker Hill* and *Bennington* flew pre–H-hour napalm and strafing attacks on the landing beach areas. It turned out to be a relatively quiet day, which could no doubt be attributed to the efforts of the preceding few days against the kamikaze bases. However, VMF-451 lost two pilots in the dawn launches, probably as the result of a join-up collision. Later in the day, all four Marine squadrons hit suspected Japanese bivouac areas and supply dumps behind the rapidly forming battle lines, as well as gun positions that were beginning to be identified.

On the second day, 2 April, both carriers flew missions similar to the first day's as the landing force continued to build up ashore, but on the third things began to get a little more active. Twelve Marine Corsairs and sixteen Hellcats from *Bunker Hill* were on an attack mission at Amami O Shima when they encountered a flight of Zekes, which seemed to have the mission of *ramming* the Corsairs. The Marines of VMF-451 shot down eleven of the enemy planes, and the Hellcats got all the rest. Second Lt. William M. Peek, Jr., got three of the Marine kills for a very successful mission.

It was not a banner day for the *Bennington* Marines, however. Fifteen Corsairs, with Hellcats from *Hornet* and *Belleau Wood* (CV 24), flew a strike mission against Hirara airfield on Miyako Island. Second Lt. Howard J. Steele, Jr., of VMF-123 was hit by antiaircraft fire over the field and had to ditch his plane about eight miles offshore. He was rescued by a handy OS2U, but unfortunately Capt. Harry J. Deal, who had helped in the rescue, was not as lucky. Deal returned to *Bennington* with the rest of the flight, but as he was preparing to land, his engine quit and he sank with his Corsair. On another mission over Ishigaki, Capt. William E. Roques of VMF-123 was also hit by AA and he too had to make a water landing. He could not jettison his canopy and went down with the plane, making it a monumentally bad day for both *Bennington* Marine squadrons.

By 6 April, the Japanese had recovered from the pre–L-day attacks on the kamikaze bases in a big way. A total of 355 suiciders were launched on the sixth and seventh, the majority of them being airborne on the sixth. This onslaught was timed with a "survivors sortie" from the Inland Sea of the last and the biggest of the enemy "battle wagons," the *Yamato*.

The horde of airborne suiciders took monstrous losses trying to penetrate the naval force's defenses. Of the more than three hundred launched on 6 April, almost 280 were shot down before reaching any targets. The great majority of these kills were by the fast carrier aircraft, with about fifty claimed by the CVE planes covering Okinawa close in and almost that many by ships' antiaircraft batteries. The *Bunker Hill* Marines were in on a part of that score as VMF-221 got twelve kills, with 2d Lt. George R. Johns getting three of them. VMF-112 and VMF-123 of *Bennington* were on CAP missions, but encountered only five of the penetrators, shooting down all five.

Even with these impressive statistics, the tragic part of the story is that twenty-two kamikazes got through the defenses. These hit twenty-two ships of varying sizes, mostly small, sinking three and causing serious damage and loss of life in many others.

The battleship *Yamato* was on a suicide mission of her own, determined to take as many as possible of the Okinawa invasion force to the bottom with her. *Yamato* was escorted by the surviving cruiser and the destroyers that were still somewhat serviceable after the carrier attacks on the Kure naval base prior to the landings at Okinawa. It was a dramatic and desperate move which literally accomplished nothing except bringing the final curtain of the war closer.

The big battleship, with the light cruiser *Yahagi* and eight destroyers, came down through Bungo and Osumi channels. They exited past the southern tip of Kyushu, and headed toward Okimawa. The *Yamato* group was tracked both from the air and by submarine. During the early searches for the enemy force, twenty-three VMF-221 Corsairs were airborne led by their skipper, Major Roberts. They ran into some "Rex" fighters and shot down five. Roberts and 1st Lt. Clay D. Haggard, Jr., got two apiece and 2d Lt. Eugene D. Cameron got a single.

In the late morning, a *Bennington* strike was partially ready for launch against the *Yamato* group. There were eleven SB2Cs, ten TBMs, seven F6Fs, and one Corsair on the flight deck, with seven other Marines sitting in their planes on the hangar deck. For some reason, now forgotten, it was decided to launch the deckload immediately and off they went. As it turned out, that particular strike group initiated the attacks on *Yamato*. The lone participating Corsair was flown by 2d Lt. Kenneth E. Huntington of VMF-112; his squadron mates had been left on the hangar deck. The flight encountered a multi-colored intense pattern of AA over the target, which Huntington raced through unscathed, planting his bomb on the forward turret of *Yamato* and silencing its guns. As Robert Sherrod paraphrased the well-known Texas Ranger quip

Bunker Hill just after taking two kamikaze hits on 11 May 1945.
Screened by destroyers, the ship is shown from a few hundred yards
to starboard as flight and hangar deck fires engulf it.

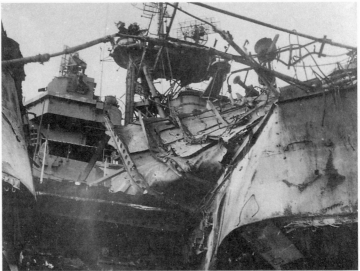

The number two elevator, where the second kamikaze hit close aboard the island structure of *Bunker Hill*.

A view of part of the flight deck of *Bunker Hill* after damage control had been restored and all fires were out. The carrier was headed for extensive repairs and its Marines for home.

from the early West: "One Marine. One bomb. One Navy Cross."

Starting shortly after noon on the seventh, a swarm of the fast carrier aircraft hit the *Yamato* task force. In the next two hours, the cruiser and four destroyers were sunk and *Yamato* had taken five bombs and ten torpedoes. At about 1430 on 7 April, she blew up with a mighty roar, rolled over, and went down. It was still a long way to V-J Day, but this symbolized to many that the end was drawing near.

The next several days were relatively routine, but on 12 April the "kamikaze korps" came with their second busiest day of the campaign. It also turned into the "biggest bag" day for the four Marine squadrons still in the fast carriers: twenty-six kills by the *Bennington* Marines and twenty-five by the Leathernecks in *Bunker Hill*. It was a very special day for Major Hansen, skipper of VMF-112: it was his twenty-fifth birthday, his three kills—in addition to his earlier ones—made him an ace, and he thus earned a Navy Cross. It was truly a banner day for this outstanding young Marine aviation leader. The twelfth of April was unofficially known in VMF-112 as "Hansen Day" (no matter how you spell it), because 1st Lt. Bert W. Hanson also got credit for two of the VMF-112 kills. Sherrod added that "the Irish got in it as well," when 1st Lt. Jack W. Callahan of VMF-112 got credit for three.

The Irish also got in it with the *Bunker Hill* Marines as Maj. Archie Donahue got five of the squadron's twenty-five kills to bring his World War II score to fourteen. Three first lieutenants of VMF-451, George S. Petersen, Raymond H. Swalley, and John R. Webb, each got two. All told it turned out to be a very good hunting day for all the Marines.

For the rest of the month it was "day in and day out, the same deal in kamikaze land"—trying to knock them down before they could penetrate and get to the ships. *Bennington* and *Bunker Hill* were successful in dodging the scourge during these days of April, but *Enterprise, Intrepid,* and several other ships of the force were hit and damaged. The carriers housing the remaining Marines did experience several near-misses, some measured in yards and inches. The kamikaze campaign wasn't a war-winning tactic, but it was psychologically effective and caused a lot of "white knuckles" when it got close.

Friday the thirteenth was a particularly bad day for VMF-123. On a strike over Kikai, antiaircraft fire hit Capt. George C. De Fabio, a Guadalcanal veteran of VMF-213, forcing him to bail out. With shore guns firing on him in the water, he could not extricate himself from the chute and was dragged under. On the same strike, 2d Lts. Franklin H. Kurchinski and Victor K. Rusling were also hit and shot down by AA and did not get out of their planes.

Although the war was moving to an end, these were very hard days for the "fleet that came to stay." Even so, from the thirteenth to the end of the month, the *Bunker Hill* Marines shot down twenty aircraft and *Bennington* VMFs were credited with ten.

The situation continued unchanged well into May. Then on the morning of the eleventh, *Bunker Hill,* Admiral Mitscher's flagship, took two kamikazes in short order—a Zeke, closely followed by a Judy.

The Zeke's pilot came out of low cloud cover, releasing his bomb just before hitting the ship himself. The plane hit the flight deck aft of the number three elevator. The bomb skidded across the flight deck, setting the parked aircraft afire. It then went through the flight deck and through the ship's side at the gallery deck level and exploded in the air, peppering the sponsons and throwing large fragments into the side.

Almost instantaneously after the Zeke hit, the Judy crashed into the flight deck close aboard the island. As with the Zeke, this one had also released its bomb just before crashing and it exploded on the gallery deck. The plane itself went through the flight deck and spewed gasoline into the gallery and hangar decks, which were instantly blazing with billowing clouds of smoke and flame at all three deck levels. In its efforts to get everything under control, *Bunker Hill* was

Captain Swett at Kadena, Okinawa, his first stop on the way home after *Bunker Hill* was hit. He was leading the airborne mission of his squadron and was eventually directed to Kadena. Note the toothbrush in his jacket pocket and his flight gear in hand.

promptly assisted by light cruiser *Wilkes-Barre* (CL 103) and three destroyers. After an hour and a half the fires on the flight deck were out, and *Wilkes-Barre* was alongside continuing to ply the hangar deck fires with all its hoses. Fires then broke out in the magazine area and the ship began a list to starboard, shut down two engines, and dropped her speed to 10 knots. After a rugged four hours, all fires were finally brought under control and steps were initiated to transfer Admiral Mitscher and the flag staff to *Enterprise.*

The total casualty count showed 389 killed or missing and 264 wounded. Included in those totals were one Marine pilot and twenty-eight enlisted Marines. An especially hard hit group was the eight air combat intelligence officers, six Navy and two Marine. Of the eight, four were killed and two badly burned, all Navy. First Lt. Leo B. Pambrun of VMF-221 went over the side and was rescued. Only 1st Lt. John E. Nayman of VMF-451 came through uninjured.

At the time the ship was hit, fifteen pilots of the two Marine squadrons were airborne on a CAP mission. They shot down four penetrators, one of them credited to Capt. James Swett, the VMF-221 executive officer who was awarded the Medal of Honor for service at Guadalcanal just over two years earlier. The flight landed aboard *Enterprise,* which also took a kamikaze hit three days later. They were only aboard a few hours, however, before they began a series of transfers which started them on the happy trek back to California.

It was the end of the war for VMF-221 and VMF-451. They were ordered home when *Bunker Hill* had to go to the rear for repairs. The two squadrons had been on board the ship for three months of almost continuous combat, during which they had shot down eighty-four enemy aircraft and destroyed many more on the ground. In numerous strafing and bombing attacks on airfields and supporting installations, they had brought extensive and irreparable damage to the Japanese. Among the costs of the two squadrons' effort were thirteen pilots—nine killed in action and four in operational accidents while aboard *Bunker Hill.*

■

The May events left Marine representation in the fast carriers to the last two squadrons, VMF-112 and VMF-123, of the *Bennington*. For another month, the "artful dodgers" of *Bennington* continued to press their luck, despite some very harrowing near misses.

On 8 June, the air group, including both Marine squadrons, was assigned an unusual mission. They were to escort the air group's bomber squadron to a familiar locale, Kanoya airfield in southern Kyushu. There, kamikaze aircraft were protected in revetments from normally fuzed bombs impacting nearby. On this mission, the SB2Cs would be carrying 500-pound bombs fuzed with VT proximity fuzes to explode them at heights of ten to forty-five feet above the ground. The idea was to spray the revetted kamikaze aircraft with bomb particles from above. Delivery was made as directed, but damage assessment was inconclusive.

Upon return to *Bennington*, the two Marine squadrons assembled in the ready room and were informed that they had just completed their last mission. The war diaries of both squadrons agree, "The cheers shook the room." That evening, the ship set course for Leyte Gulf where the Marines would start the happy journey homeward.

From 16 February to 8 June, the two *Bennington* squadrons had put together a remarkable and exceptional set of combat statistics:

Combat sorties	2,554
Total hours flown	12,047
Enemy planes shot down	82
Enemy planes destroyed on ground	149
Tons of bombs dropped	102.7
Rockets fired	4,097
Rounds of .50 cal fired	933,991
Gallons of napalm dropped	8,250

Marine Fighter Squadrons 112 and 123 lost thirty-one Corsairs in combat and seventeen more in operational accidents.

Forty-one planes damaged were transferred and a total of fifty-four replacement aircraft were received on board.

The costs of this combat period were not light. Eighteen pilots—one in three of the original roster on boarding *Bennington*—were lost. Fifteen more were rescued after being shot or forced down.

The relief of the *Bennington* Marine squadrons brought this episode of Marine Corps carrier operations to a close. It was a highly commendable though costly performance, executed under the pressures and critical urgencies of a nation at war.

There are many lessons of value that came out of these Marines' experience during the Pacific campaign of World War II. Most of these lessons have been well absorbed by the Navy and Marine Corps over the decades that followed. Evolving technological changes have been constant and continuous in aircraft carriers and all the equipment and systems that have maintained their unique effectiveness over the years. There are two lasting points that remain applicable to current technological states and times, and perhaps well into the future, that bear emphasizing, however.

First, this was an interservice assignment of forces within the Department of the Navy that *could only be accepted.* In this case, the only way the fighter performance of the fast carrier air groups could be increased *immediately* was by ordering Marine Corsairs onto carriers. It should be remembered that in national emergencies, this type of "no option" assignments can, and will, occur.

Second, the commonalities of training, pilot assignments, and service equipment between Navy and Marine Corps aviation within the Department of the Navy are the factors that made such an emergency reinforcement possible. This is precisely as set forth, as of 1939, in the Marine aviation mission statement cited in the introduction. This flexibility of command within naval aviation should be well remembered as a major Department of Defense asset as the future unfolds.

5   The Carrier Escort Program

USS *Block Island* (CVE 106)

COMMANDING OFFICER
Capt. Francis Massie Hughes

MARINE CARRIER AIR GROUP 1
Lt. Col. John H. Dobbin

MARINE FIGHTER SQUADRON 511
Maj. Robert C. Maze to 27 May
Capt. James L. Secrest from 28 May

MARINE TORPEDO BOMBER SQUADRON 233
Capt. Edmund W. Berry

USS *Gilbert Islands* (CVE 107)

COMMANDING OFFICER
Capt. Lester K. Rice

MARINE CARRIER AIR GROUP 3
Lt. Col. William R. Campbell

MARINE FIGHTER SQUADRON 512
Maj. Blaine H. Baesler

MARINE TORPEDO BOMBER SQUADRON 143
Capt. John E. Worlund

USS *Vella Gulf* (CVE 111)

COMMANDING OFFICER
Capt. Robert W. Morse

MARINE CARRIER AIR GROUP 3
Lt. Col. Royce W. Coln

MARINE FIGHTER SQUADRON 513
Lt. Col. Thomas O. Bales

MARINE TORPEDO BOMBER SQUADRON 234
Capt. Edward J. Montagne

USS *Cape Gloucester* (CVE 109)

COMMANDING OFFICER
Capt. John W. Harris

MARINE CARRIER AIR GROUP 4
Lt. Col. Donald K. Yost

MARINE FIGHTER SQUADRON 351
Maj. Armond H. DeLalio

MARINE TORPEDO BOMBER SQUADRON 132
Capt. Henry H. Hise

The Marine Corps escort carrier program, as mentioned briefly in the introduction, stemmed from the post-Tarawa recommendation by Gen. Holland M. Smith, early in 1944. Analyses after Tarawa had shown that there was dissatisfaction with the close air support of the landing force in the operation. *History of the U. S. Marine Corps Operations in World War II*, volume V, *Victory and Occupation,* states the case briefly.

At Tarawa, defense against air attack and the close support of ground troops were both entrusted to carrier planes flown by Navy pilots. In the opinion of both Navy and Marine officers, the air support at Tarawa left much to be desired in the way of accomplishment. Many apparent shortcomings in this operation indicated that, among other things, truly effective air support was impossible unless the pilots and ground troops had trained as a team.

After the operation, General Smith recommended that "Marine aviators, thoroughly schooled in the principles of direct air support," should do the job. Smith maintained they should operate from carriers and be included in any future amphibious operation undertaken by a Marine division. He further recommended that if this request could not be granted, "the Navy airmen selected for the task should be carefully indoctrinated in the tactics they would employ."

The overall fleet demands for carriers continued to grow through 1944 as the offensive toward Japan gained momentum. The accompanying heavy demands on the entire training structure added up to the fact that the Navy high command could not approve Smith's request at that stage of the war. The subject was considered repeatedly both in Washington and in the Pacific through the first six or seven months of the year, but the situation remained unchanged.

In late July Gen. Alexander A. Vandegrift, Commandant of the Marine Corps, accompanied by several key staff officers, made an inspection trip to the Pacific. It culminated in a three-day conference with Adm. Chester W. Nimitz, commander in chief of the Pacific fleet (CinCPac), at Honolulu. Many items were on the agenda, but the decisions reached finally included approval of a Marine CVE program, specifically geared to the close air support of Marines landing in the amphibious assault.

The initial form of the program was structured around a six-ship carrier division, each CVE to have a Marine carrier air group (MCVG). The MCVG would consist of two squadrons: an eighteen-plane fighter squadron and a twelve-plane torpedo bomber squadron. The squadron designations would also be slightly changed, to VMF(CVS) and VMTB (CVS), to indicate they were specially trained and assigned to the CVE program. A Marine carrier aircraft service detach-

ment (CASD) would be assigned to each CVE for maintenance of the MCVG aircraft and for other "housekeeping"
chores associated with the MCVG operations aboard the
ship.

The carriers were to be the latest design of CVE, the *Com-
mencement Bay* (CVE 105) class. The fighter aircraft would be
the F4U Corsair with some F6F Hellcats for night fighter and
photoreconnaissance work. The torpedo bomber would be
the TBF/TBM Avenger, configured to be fully rocket-capable.

A further result of the decisions reached at the conference
was the provision that a "Marine aviator of suitable rank"
would be given the responsibility to organize and prepare the
MCVGs for carrier operations. He would head a command
known as Marine Carrier Groups Pacific, with headquarters at MCAS Santa Barbara, and with a major activity of
the command at MCAS Mojave, California. Col. Albert D.
Cooley was assigned to this post at Santa Barbara and also to
the command of Marine Air Support Group 48 (MASG-48).
The author was assigned as his executive officer. MASG-
48 consisted of the headquarters and two of the MCVGs at
Santa Barbara, while MASG-51 at Mojave had the other four
MCVGs, as they were assigned. Originally, the commands
were organized this way with the intention of assigning the
four MCVGs at Mojave to the first four CVEs ready for deployment; the two at Santa Barbara were scheduled to be replacement MCVGs.

There were other associated decisions made to get more
Marine personnel into the control of direct support operations in amphibious operations, but essentially the CVE program began as depicted above. By the time the first elements
of the program were in place, however, changes were required.

In his final approval of the program in the fall of 1944,
Admiral King, CominCh, stated, "A sufficient number of
squadrons were to be trained in carrier operations to permit
an ultimate total of sixteen CVE groups to be embarked
simultaneously [emphasis added], and to furnish adequate

spare groups." This was to be accomplished by February 1946. Yet by the time Colonel Cooley established Marine Carrier Groups Pacific at Santa Barbara on 21 October 1944, changes were beginning to alter program levels visualized by Admiral King, as the war situation altered from that estimated at the time of the CinCPac conference between Nimitz and Vandegrift.

Before the end of the conflict, the projected total number of MCVGs was considerably reduced, and only four actually deployed before V-J Day. Of the four, only the first three actually got out in time to see some combat action, the fourth arriving simultaneously with the end of the war. Several other MCVGs were formed and in training at the end of the war, but did not see action. An important precedent had been established with the approval of these MCVGs, however. It was a favorable portent for improved direct support of Marines in future amphibious operations, which was realized as early as 1950 at Inchon in the Korean War.

A vital concern in the training of all four of the MCVGs was the inculcation of carrier techniques and the operational basics of life on a floating platform. Since the majority of the pilots had had practically none of this coverage in their flight training, there was a lot to do in a short time. Carrier training was made all the more crucial by the fact that the Corsair had only a limited history in carrier aviation—all on the fast carriers. The Corsair had not fared as well as the F6F Hellcat in earlier suitability trials in late 1943, when the Navy chose the Hellcat as the standard fleet fighter. Furthermore, the CVE 105–class carrier was slower, and had a much narrower and shorter flight deck, than the basic fleet carrier of the CV 9 class.

The first carrier ready for the program was the *Block Island* (CVE 106). She bore a distinguished name in the ships annals of the Navy in World War II. *Block Island* (CVE 21) was the only ship lost in the antisubmarine warfare of the Atlantic against the Germans that was reincarnated in Pacific combat against the Japanese. She achieved further distinction when the commanding officer and almost all of the Atlantic crew survivors were ordered to man the new *Block Island* (CVE 106) in the Pacific. Continuing her long list of unusual historic characteristics, she also became the first carrier of any class to be assigned an all-Marine air group.

The commanding officer of both the Atlantic and the Pacific *Block Islands* was Capt. Francis Massie Hughes, an early carrier pilot with a great deal of experience in the prewar operations of naval aviation in addition to his World War II combat in the Atlantic. After losing his first ship, Captain Hughes was determined to get a new ship named *Block Island,* and his persistent pursuit of that objective was directly responsible for his move to the Pacific with his surviving crew.

When the ship was commissioned on 30 December 1944, the new *Block Island*'s designated sponsor was Mrs. E. J. Hallenbeck, the mother of Marine ace Pappy Boyington—at the time still listed as missing in action and not yet known to be a prisoner of the Japanese. Early in February, MCVG-1 and CASD-1 reported aboard and the Marine CVE program was under way.

Like the *Block Island,* MCVG-1 was loaded from the top down with combat-experienced leadership in all categories. Lt. Col. John H. Dobbin, the air group commander, was a fighter ace from early Guadalcanal. Dobbin was the first to launch from the *Block Island* and also the first to land aboard when he brought his Corsair around the pattern for his initial landing. Dobbin's fighter and torpedo bomber squadron commanders were also combat veterans from the Battle of Midway and the Solomons. Each squadron had combat-knowledgeable pilots in key positions to help train the rest, who were largely just out of the flight training command. Although the majority of MCVG-1 pilots were going to combat for the first time, under such a leadership structure the prospects for seasoned training beforehand were very positive.

The MCVGs that deployed later were structured in similar leadership patterns as that described for MCVG-1—a capable nucleus of combat experience with which to train the less experienced majority of the squadron pilots. Lt. Cols. William R. Campbell of MCVG-2, Donald K. Yost of MCVG-4, and Royce W. Coln of MCVG-3, and each of their squadron commanders, were all Solomons veterans in the type of aircraft with which their squadrons were equipped.

A unique aspect of the *Block Island*/MCVG-1 team was the fact that the ship had a special height-finding radar to be used in controlling night fighter operations. Because of this, one squadron, VMF(CVS)-511, was being equipped with only eight F4U Corsairs in order to make room for eight F6F-5N night fighter Hellcats and two F6F-5P photo aircraft. This slightly complicated the supply and maintenance picture, but it did provide the planned CVE division with night fighter and reconnaissance capabilities. The F6Fs were all flown by Marines trained in the same manner and in the same schools as the Navy night fighter and photo specialists. The other MCVGs deployed with Corsairs only in their fighter squadrons.

MCVG-1 was the first group to join its designated CVE, complete its training, qualify aboard, and deploy. During initial training on *Block Island* off the California coast, however, a tragic incident gave MCVG-1 a very rocky start. A mixed flight was launched in spite of very uncertain weather conditions. After the launch, the weather worsened markedly, and by the time recall was given, the entire area—both at sea and inland—was fogged in. The result was disaster.

Of the eleven aircraft in the launch—five TBMs, four Corsairs, and two F6Fs—only one TBM was able to land aboard the ship after recall. The others could not see the ship well enough to enter the landing pattern safely. They were directed to land either at the San Nicolas Island airstrip or aboard *Ranger* (CV 4), which was operating in the area. Of the ten that did not return to the ship, two F6Fs landed safely in almost zero-zero weather at Santa Barbara. The remaining eight were lost, having either ditched at sea or crashed attempting to land at San Nicolas or elsewhere. Two pilots and four crewmen of VMTB-233, including the squadron commander, were killed. Two of the TBMs made water landings, with the crews fortunately being rescued.

Under the leadership of Lieutenant Colonel Dobbin, the tragedy, as shattering as it was, was not permitted to blight the initiation of the Marine CVE program. Training was resumed and a team relationship with the ship's company was preserved. A formal investigation of the incident was held (the author was a member of the board) with no specific responsibility assigned.

The main cause was attributed to the extremely quick and unusual blanketing of the entire coast with an impenetrable layer of fog down to "zero" level over both the land and sea.

Within this whole disastrous episode there is an interesting historical aviation factor that is worthy of comment. It is derived from the one TBM that returned to the ship and the two night fighters that landed safely at Santa Barbara.

The TBM was flown by 1st Lt. Albert G. Schoneberger, the assistant flight officer of VMTB-233. He had been an instructor in TBF/TBM aircraft in the training command prior to reporting to the squadron, and had accumulated close to a thousand hours in the Avenger. Schoneberger was keenly aware of the values of the Link trainer, the flight simulator of World War II times, in learning instrument flying and all its procedures. His normal duties in the squadron included making out daily flight schedules, and also assignments for both scheduled times in the Link trainer and for instrument training flights as well. The Link was "kind of jerky" in some of its movements and pilots generally tried to avoid as many Link "hops" as possible, preferring to spend their time on the ground in other pursuits. When this happened, Schoneberger would take the vacated Link time if he wasn't flying. As a result he had plenty of practice and learned precisely the procedures for homing on the radio device known as the ZB/YG or "hay rig." This is what brought him back aboard promptly on the night of the tragedy.

Similar proficiency also brought the two F6F-5Ns into Santa Barbara in the same very bad weather and visibility conditions. World War II night fighter pilots acquired an immediate and keen appreciation for instrument flying and all its procedures on their entry into their specialized training. Today, in the jet age, instrument proficiency is an absolute requirement for tactical flight operations. Simulators are a valuable "must" in today's high-tech, high-speed aviation environment. They are no longer considered something to be avoided, as they regrettably were to a damaging degree in World War II times.

Capt. Edmund W. Berry succeeded to command of VMTB (CVS)-233 and, together with Maj. Robert C. Maze of VMF (CVS)-511, the two squadron commanders resumed readiness training with a will under the firm hand of Colonel Dobbin. All pilots of MCVG-1 got eight initial qualification landings aboard the ship, and by the time *Block Island* deployed about seven weeks later, the average number of landings per pilot was at a much higher "comfort level." With rocket, bombing, and gunnery training on ranges in the San Diego and inland areas, the group felt ready to "go get 'em" by 20 March when the ship sortied from San Diego for Hawaii and beyond.

With further night qualification and other training exercises in the Hawaiian area, the final polish was put on the MCVG-1 preparation. *Block Island* sortied for Ulithi in company with *Harry E. Hubbard* (DD 748) as Task Unit 12.5.2. Marine Carrier Air Group 1 was on board at its full strength of forty-five pilot officers and thirty aircraft, ready for combat.

On 28 April, within eighteen miles of Ulithi, word was received that an enemy aircraft had penetrated the area. *Block Island* went to general quarters. The CIC (combat information center) team watched on its radar plot as shore-based fighters intercepted and shot down the intruder. The enemy plane crashed a short distance from *Block Island,* and some of the interceptors came near the ship trying to indicate the crash site. When they did not identify themselves properly, the ship 40-mm batteries opened up. The effect was a noisy "welcome to the war" for the first of the 105-class CVEs. The ship retrieved some debris and remains of the downed aircraft and identified them definitely as Japanese. Not many enemy aircraft penetrated the vast area of the Ulithi anchorage at that time, so it was a "special show" almost in honor of the arrival of *Block Island* and MCVG-1. Okinawa, where they would soon be, was several hundred miles farther on, but this initial event made all hands feel that they were getting very close to the action.

On 3 May, *Block Island* rendezvoused with Task Unit 52.1.1, the escort carrier group, under Rear Adm. Calvin T. Durgin about sixty-five miles southeast of Okinawa, and Captain Hughes reported her ready for action. It was the first look the escort carrier group had at a 105-class CVE. To the smaller and war-weary Kaiser shipyard–class CVEs, the *Block Island* looked pretty good—almost *big.*

Rear Admiral Durgin was in command of all the escort carriers at Okinawa. His attitude toward the arrival of MCVGs into his domain was surprising, to say the least. Regarding the specialized training of the Marine CVE concept, Admiral Durgin declared:

It must be remembered that CVEG and VC squadrons are similarly specially trained. The advent of Marine Air Groups in CVEs should not be permitted to complicate the support carrier picture any more than is necessary. . . . Marine Air Groups should be and probably are as flexible as Navy squadrons and groups, and should remain so, and should expect no preferential treatment. *To assign all Marine squadrons to direct support work would probably work to the detriment of morale of the Navy groups and squadrons* [emphasis added] and this command sees at the present writing no reason for such assignments and has no intention of allowing it to occur.

Reproduction of an annotated target aerial photo, which shows part of the complex of kamikaze bases in the Sakishima Gunto. The enemy would fly in the kamikazes from bases in Formosa late in the day before the planned attack. They would take off for the Okinawa area beginning at first light. Since at least five fields are seen in this single aerial photo presentation, a significant number of suiciders could mount out of this one island on any given day.

This was an unfortunate turn of events for the concept of the Marine CVE program in its initial stages. No request had ever been voiced for any "preferential treatment." The concept of the program was aimed at improvement of the direct air support of the landing forces of the amphibious assault. It warranted a maximum trial for the campaign then in preparation—Operation Olympic, the assault on the home islands of Japan. This was not forthcoming, however, and Admiral Durgin's apparent inability to understand why Marine CVE air groups were being deployed is difficult to comprehend at best. It was not exactly a "welcome aboard" message.

In spite of the decisions reached by his superiors in structuring the Marine CVE program, the MCVGs were only sparsely used as they were trained and intended to be employed—in support of Marines ashore. MCVG-1 would have only eight days of direct support of Marines on Okinawa, MCVG-2 only five, and MCVG-4 none. By the time the high command overruled Admiral Durgin, the war had come to an end. The concept of the Marine CVE program would not be fully validated until Korea at Pusan and Inchon in 1950, and in the later phases of the Korean war as well.

Once in the Okinawa theater, MCVG-1 wasted no time in going to work on what it had been waiting for. The first couple of days were on a sort of "breaking in" set of missions, primarily local CAP and antisubmarine patrols. These missions were more or less uneventful. But early on the third day of its arrival at Okinawa, things of greater interest began to show up.

The fifth of May started with a morning rocket and bomb strike on an enemy strongpoint near Naha by VMTB-233, and followed up through midday with a fighter strafe of installations on a very small offshore island. In the mid-afternoon a sizable strike was launched against Sakishima Gunto, a strong kamikaze base complex 175 miles southwest of Okinawa. With the CAG leading eight Corsairs in escort of eight Avengers, the strike hit Hirara and Nobara airfields, cratering

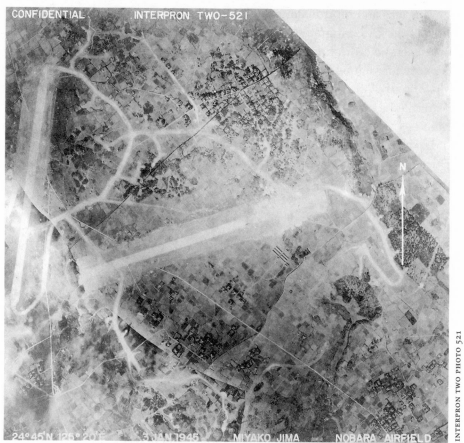

Nobara Airfield on Miyako Jima was a tough, well-defended spot.

runways, rocketing buildings, and strafing all installations. There was no air opposition and very few usable aircraft evident on the fields, but Colonel Dobbin reported that the antiaircraft fire was intense and accurate. The enemy gunners had had plenty of practice—since the escort carrier group had been working the place over for several weeks—"and they showed it," said Dobbin.

One Avenger failed to return and 2d Lt. Douglas M. Herrin, Staff Sgt. Edward T. Gunning, and Sgt. Joseph L. Butehorn were declared missing in action when no trace of them was found by air/sea rescue aircraft. Several other planes were hit, but all got back to the carrier without incident, except one. Capt. Frank Takacs of VMTB-233 had to ditch his TBM alongside *Butler* (DD 636) on return to the ship because of heavy damage to the landing gear and loss of hydraulic pressure. Takacs and his two crewmen were fortunate; they were immediately rescued and were back aboard *Block Island* before nightfall. During the strike, the Hellcat photo aircraft of VMF-511 also got into action, making repeated runs to get the reconnaissance coverage required by the CVE division command.

A British carrier force had joined the U.S. fleet off Okinawa about the same time *Block Island* arrived in the area. An arrangement was set up during May, which had the Royal Navy aircraft striking Sakishima Gunto 9, 12, and 15 May, while the Americans attacked it 10, 11, 13, 14, and so on. This created an opportunity for MCVG-1 to fly missions in support of the Marine divisions on the ground on the days it was not required to attack Sakishima. These missions were mixed with CAP, however, so MCVG-1 did not provide as much close air support in front of the ground Marines "as we would have liked," in the words of Lieutenant Colonel Dobbin, and certainly not as much as conceived in the original plan of the Marine CVE program.

On 15 May, in an attack on Hirara airfield on Miyako Island, 1st Lt. Edward J. Wallof of VMF-511 sustained a direct hit on his cockpit canopy. The shattering fragments of plexiglass slashed his left eye severely, but he continued his rocket run and pulled out successfully. By then his wounds had almost blinded him, but one of his squadron mates, flying close formation on him, coached him the hundred miles back to the ship and into his landing approach. Wallof was able to land successfully and safely aboard.

As the Marine divisions pushed southward during the month, they met stubborn resistance centered around Shuri Castle, an ancient Okinawan walled fortress. The walls around parts of Shuri were several feet thick and very resistant to artillery fire. On the twenty-fourth, Avengers of VMTB-233 were loaded with 2,000-pound bombs with delayed fuzes, and made a low level skip-bombing attack against the walls. A successful breach was achieved, which enabled the ground Marines to eventually take the area and continue the advance.

On the twenty-seventh, VMF(CVS)-511 suffered an unfortunate loss when the squadron skipper, Major Maze, was shot down during an attack on enemy shipping near Ishigaki Island. He was leading a rocket run and went straight into the water just offshore, undoubtedly heavily hit by AA. No trace was found in later searches. Capt. James L. Secrest, an aggressive Guadalcanal veteran, succeeded Maze as commanding officer of VMF-511.

Secrest later characterized the enemy antiaircraft fire at Miyako and Ishigaki, particularly from small arms, as being "the deadliest I had flown against." He noted that it compared closely to the flak thrown up by an enemy battleship he had attacked off Guadalcanal. He also commented that there was a lack of tracer ammunition in the small-arms loading. As a result, the first a pilot realized he was being fired on was "when holes appeared in your wing or your canopy was hit!"

Amami O Shima was no different in intensity and accuracy of antiaircraft fire. The author subsequently had an opportunity to see why both Amami and Sakishima were so effective. One of the surrender conditions required the Japanese to uncover all camouflage from gun positions immediately after V-J Day. When this was done, the sheer number of antiaircraft weapons was unbelievable. Gun pits were tangential down the entire length of ridge lines and far exceeded what had been detected through the camouflage. In spite of the fact that Amami O Shima and Sakishima Gunto were subjected to almost daily aerial photography coverage during the Okinawa operation, as well as during strikes, most of the gun emplacements were not suspected.

The rest of May was a continuation of the same variation of missions, although there were some very significant developments. One of these was the arrival of MCVG-2 in *Gilbert Islands* on the twenty-first. Initially attached to Task Unit 52.1.1, Colonel Campbell and MCVG-2 started operations against the enemy in a similar pattern to that experienced by Colonel Dobbin's air group. MCVG-2 began with strikes on Sakishima Gunto and were soon introduced to the much-practiced enemy antiaircraft sharpshooters at Ishigaki and Miyako. Like MCVG-1, they also got a chance to perform their specialty—Marine close air support—but were only able to do five days in their entire deployment, as mentioned earlier. As Colonel Campbell put it politely in referring to Admiral Durgin, "He just seemed opposed to the idea of Marine Carrier Air Groups."

On 23 May, MCVG-2 had its first casualty when 2d Lt. Edgar T. Miller crashed into the sea about ten miles astern of the carrier. On the same day, Maj. Elton Mueller had a bad landing and hit a parked Corsair forward, taking it over the starboard side with his own aircraft. Fortunately he was rescued quickly by the plane guard *Helm* (DD 388) and was returned to the ship uninjured.

Mueller, an excellent pilot ashore, was an interesting example of what happens very rarely in operations at sea: he was subject to chronic seasickness, regardless of weather or sea state. All through the training period at sea before deployment, Mueller struggled with his ailment, giving it an extreme try and for short periods was getting by in excellent shape. Permanent residence aboard ship, however, with little inclination to eat and very limited sleep made it impossible. Fortunately, the result was not an operational statistic. Colonel Campbell arranged to have him transferred to the Marine aviation command at Okinawa and after a short time on terra firma, he was assigned to command a fighter squadron there. He did very well in all aspects of his assignment and compiled a fine record ashore.

MCVG-2 suffered its first combat loss at Ishigaki when a TBM was heavily hit and set afire. The pilot was able to keep it airborne to a point about ten miles to seaward before he was forced to ditch. First Lt. Robert B. Cromwell and Cpl. Robert L. Wood were rescued, but Staff Sgt. William C. Boyd went down with the plane.

On the last day of the month, Capt. Thomas Liggett, Jr., of VMF-512, bagged the first enemy aircraft for *Gilbert Islands*. Liggett had been an early Guadalcanal dive-bomber pilot and was credited there with a direct hit on an enemy transport during the toughest of the early days. He converted to fighters at Samoa in 1944 and his conversion was a resounding success. Liggett was leading four Corsairs on a CAP flight when the controllers reported a single at high altitude. He was vectored toward the bogey and climbed with his flight to check it out. On reaching the altitude the "meatballs" were immediately visible. Although Liggett felt he was at too long a range, he let go with all six machine guns and "the darn thing blew up!" Just to be sure, Liggett followed the enemy plane all the way down to the water and saw it go in. It was a great morale-building performance for MCVG-2, the squadron, the ship, and all hands. The enemy bird was a twin-engine "Dinah," either on reconnaissance or a would-be kamikaze mission—in either case, an abject failure.

Lieutenant Colonel Campbell was not entirely happy with the operational relationships aboard *Gilbert Islands*. While he observed that everyone from Captain Rice on down was pleasant in demeanor and general attitude toward MCVG-2,

A VMF-512 Corsair approaches the ramp of *Gilbert Islands* on completion of a mission en route to Okinawa.

Second Lt. Jack G. Moss looks weary after his 8.7-hour-long mission in a Corsair cockpit—his first strike to Kyushu.

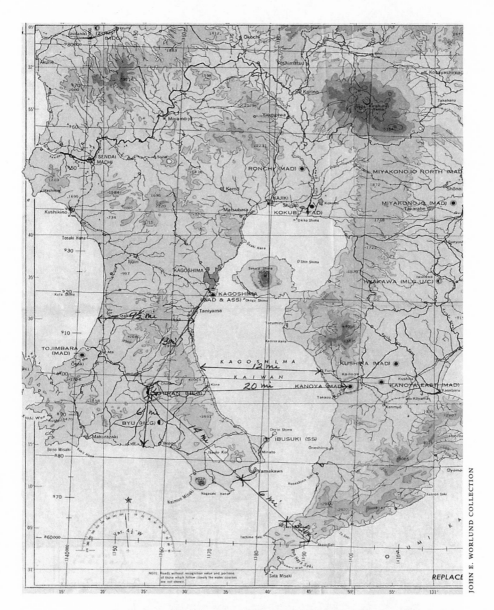

A portion of a chart of southern Kyushu, the locale of many missions assigned to the Marine CVE air groups off Okinawa. Note the distance annotations the pilots habitually added as quick decision-making aids in the event of emergencies. A prime objective, if one was seriously hit, was to make a water landing in open sea areas as far from enemy shores as possible, making air-sea rescue (ASR) feasible.

a shortage of operating carrier experience was noticeable. The captain had qualified aboard *Langley* (CV 1) in the 1920s but had not spent much time aboard CVs since. This lack of familiarity with the "nuts and bolts" of carrier operations in the top echelons of the ship carried through both the executive officer and the air officer.

The effect, in Colonel Campbell's view, was a doubtful or almost unwilling attitude toward anything beyond conservative, tried-and-true tactics. For example, this resulted in an unwillingness to utilize the Tiny Tim 11.75-inch rockets, which were on board and which MCVG-2 had been trained in, presumably because of the *Franklin* disaster. Campbell believed these would have been most effective in any attack of Japanese naval vessels, as well as against the walls of Shuri Castle ashore on Okinawa. In both instances, Tiny Tims were proposed by the CAG but declined by the *Gilbert Islands* command.

Another example of an apparent lack of operational understanding created an operating hazard whenever several carriers were operating together. It evolved from the failure of the ship to make clear to the carrier task group that the Corsair speed and turning radius required more distance between the smaller CVEs and the CVE 105 class when operating on parallel courses. This was repeatedly pointed out to *Gilbert Islands* by Campbell, but nothing was ever done to accommodate the differences in FM Wildcat (the smaller CVE air group fighter) and Corsair patterns around the ships. The result was often an uncomfortably dangerous, overlapping, and crowded air space for both launch and recovery of aircraft. To the Marines it seemed a few hundred yards more of separation abeam for 105-class CVEs and their smaller "buddies" would not have significantly degraded the task unit defense integrity against enemy air attack.

On 1 June, *Gilbert Islands* joined *Block Island* in Task Unit 32.1.3 and at last the two Marine air groups were together. This was approaching the original employment concept and was a step toward the basic Pacific fleet organization wherein both carriers were already units, on paper, of Carrier Division 27. Unfortunately, Adm. Dixwell Ketcham still had his flag at San Diego and Carrier Division 27 would not make it into action until about six weeks prior to V-J Day.

For the first half of June, the two air groups worked the routine of two days against the Sakishima Gunto complex to the southwest of Okinawa or Amami O Shima to the northeast, followed by a third day in support of the troops ashore. These missions were shared with the Navy CVE air groups and, in the case of the Sakishima complex, with the British carrier task group.

In mid-June *Block Island* and *Gilbert Islands* were pulled out of the Okinawa CVE force and sent back to Leyte Gulf on a special mission. This time it was at least *related* to the mission originally approved by CinCPac, but the mission was still a departure from the basic concept of supporting their fellow Marines in amphibious assault operations. Instead, they would support Australian ground troops in an amphibious landing to secure Balikpapan in Borneo, Netherlands East Indies.

The two CVEs were organized with a Navy CVE air group in *Suwannee* (CVE 27) as the supporting close air support force for the landing. The force arrived off the objective area just prior to the scheduled D-day of 1 July. The Thirteenth Air Force had been hitting the objective area for three weeks and a naval task force had been shelling it for two. As a result there was only light opposition at the beaches on D-day.

Because of faulty communications and lack of effective air-ground teamwork, a Navy strike rocketed and bombed some captured barracks that the landing force troops had neglected to report to the CVE command. In this unfortunate incident, several soldiers were killed, and as a result, the Australian division adopted a policy of not using close air support. This left the CVE force with nothing to do except look for targets of opportunity. This development made the whole assignment something of a disappointment, with a couple of exceptions.

For *Block Island* and MCVG-1, the exception was the appearance of the lone enemy aircraft opposing the entire operation, a Jake floatplane that came into the area just after midnight early on D+2. First Lt. Bruce J. Reuter of VMF (CVS)-511 was on CAP over the objective area in his trusty F6F-5N. Fighter direction from *Block Island* vectored Reuter into position and he disposed of the intruding Jake with his first burst, sending it spinning down in flames. Just a case of "one intruder, one Hellcat"—and one shot in the arm for force morale.

The *Gilbert Islands* and MCVG-2 exception was more devastating to the retreating Japanese and allowed participation by more of the air group. Colonel Campbell was leading a mixed strike group of forty-eight planes from the force when they spotted a large convoy of troops, vehicles, and heavy equipment moving out of the beachhead area, about thirty miles inland on a narrow road. Campbell directed attacks on both ends of the column and brought it to a complete stop. From there, the bombing, rocketing, and strafing took "complete charge," wreaking total destruction. In Campbell's words, "We shot off everything we had and wished we had more!" It was one of those dream missions and resulted in a big loss to the retreating enemy forces.

On 4 July, *Block Island* and *Gilbert Islands* were ordered back to Leyte Gulf, where Colonel Cooley reported aboard *Block Island* as commanding officer of Marine Air Support Group 48. Although not recorded in the historical records that are available today, it seems reasonably certain that discussions occurred at this point between Colonel Cooley and Admiral Durgin. The approved concept of the program was so much at variance with the deployment experience of the MCVGs, it is inconceivable that the subject was not reviewed in detail and recorded accordingly.

Block Island was subsequently ordered to Guam and saw no further combat. *Gilbert Islands* was sent to Ulithi in mid-July, and about 1 August, shortly before the end of the war, was ordered to the support group for Task Force 58 south of Japan.

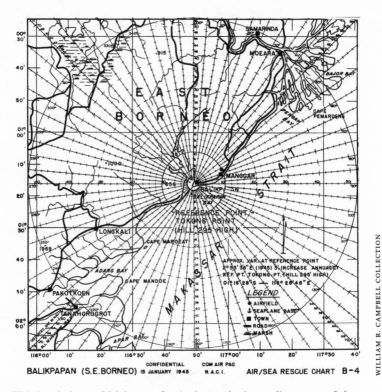

This local chart of Makassar Strait shows the immediate area of the Balikpapan, Borneo, landing of the 7th Australian Division on 1 July 1945. The landing was supported by MCVG-1 and MCVG-2 through 2 July.

First Lt. Bruce J. Reuter is shown in his trusty F6F-5N after the VMF-511 pilot returned from his first night kill at Borneo. His pride and pleasure in the new victory insignia on his fighter is obvious.

The last two MCVGs to deploy were both proceeding with steady progress at Santa Barbara and Mojave as the months of 1945 rolled by. By the end of April, MCVG-3 and MCVG-4 were approaching the last phases of their training schedules. Keyed to the CVE 105 production schedules, the readiness of the MCVGs and the CASDs were generally compatible with the completion dates of the ships. In the spring of 1945 MCVG-4 was assigned to *Cape Gloucester* (CVE 109) and MCVG-3 was slated for *Vella Gulf* (CVE 111).

With the war beginning to wind down, these would be the final two MCVGs of the program to deploy for the combat zone. MCVG-4 and CASD-4 joined *Cape Gloucester* late in April and by 23 May departed San Diego for Pearl Harbor. The ship arrived in Hawaii on 30 May and spent two weeks in the area putting the final touches on the training of both ship and air group.

Much of this time was spent practicing gunnery against drone targets launched from the flight deck. This made it an indoctrination for all hands as all calibers—from the .50 caliber machine guns through the 20-mm guns—blasted away at the drones as they made their radio-controlled passes. The "five inchers" on the fantail were the last batteries to bear as the drones made their run from bow to stern. However, they often had trouble picking up the drone, and before they could acquire the little target, the "cease firing" alarm would sound. The gunner's comment was simply, "We have to see it before we can hit it." On one occasion, a drone malfunction gave a very realistic touch to "kamikaze indoctrination" when it looped back after being shot off the catapult and crashed on the flight deck, fortunately with no damage to ship or crew. The noise of the forties, twenties, and fifties blasting away at the drones let the crew know that the ship was about to set course for "the sound of the guns."

For MCVG-4 the time in Hawaiian waters was spent in final smoothing up of flight operations around the ship. No time was wasted in getting to this final training of the air group. On 1 June the ship put to sea for night operations. The night familiarization was important, but it proved to be expensive to VMF(CVS)-351. Maj. Armond H. DeLalio, the squadron commander, suffered a barrier engagement resulting in his Corsair flipping over on its back. The initial determination of a possible injury to his spine was at first thought to be inconsequential, but continued tests showed a fracture of two vertebrae. As a result, Major DeLalio was hospitalized and relieved by his executive officer, Maj. Charles E. McLean, Jr.

On a following night familiarization mission, Capt. Frederick S. Rowe, Jr., and 2d Lt. William N. Scheer failed to return to the ship. Since there were no radio transmissions from either pilot and the results of a search effort mounted at daylight were negative, it was assumed that a midair collision was the probable cause. The night qualification period was completed without further incident and the ship returned to Pearl on 5 June.

The nature of night operations of both the Corsairs and the Avengers from the CVE were considered barely marginal, in the general view of the pilots of both types. The main factors generating this opinion were related to the CVE's design limitations. The problems of deck size and ship's characteristics, which were merely "difficulties" in daylight operations, became almost prohibitive of effective night operations.

After about two weeks in Hawaiian waters, *Cape Gloucester* departed for Leyte Gulf, arriving there 29 June. It turned out to be a very short stay as orders came in for the ship to depart Leyte on 1 July to proceed to the South China Sea. The mission was to cover a group of minesweepers at work clearing enemy minefields. For the first few days, the mission turned out to be one CAP hop after another for the fighters, plus a series of equally monotonous scouting and antisubmarine missions for the TBM "turkies." But soon, business picked up rapidly.

The action began on the twentieth with the first-ever enemy aircraft bagged by the ship when 1st Lt. Philip E. Fuller brought down a Kate reconnaissance aircraft while on CAP. It was also Fuller's first score and turned into a celebration of ship, air group, and all hands. Fuller landed last when the flight returned to the ship, where a good portion of the ship's company was waiting to welcome him with a rousing salute. Capt. John W. Harris had him report to the bridge for congratulations and in a very few minutes there was a "rising sun" decal affixed to the bridge in a prominent spot. It was a bonafide morale booster for, what up to that time, had seemed almost like the doldrums.

Three days later on another CAP mission, 1st Lt. Carroll R. Vogelaar was a member of a four-plane CAP mission when another Kate entered the area. "Moose," as he was known to his squadron mates in VMF(CVS)-351, was a big, 225-pound outgoing Marine who had become well known and popular on the *Cape Gloucester* since MCVG-4 had reported aboard. When the flight was vectored onto the intruding Kate, the enemy pilot headed out of the area at full throttle. In the ensuing chase Vogelaar finally got within range at a spot about forty miles from the ship. He wanted to make sure of his target so he closed to point blank range directly astern and his first burst exploded the enemy plane, with pieces of the wreckage hitting Vogelaar's Corsair, fortunately with no serious damage. On return to the ship, with due ceremony, a second rising sun decal joined the first on the "*Cape G*" bridge.

The following morning the CAG, Lieutenant Colonel Yost, was up on an early CAP mission and encountered a lone "Val" dive-bomber en route across the East China Sea at 20,000 feet. With no idea of letting this one get away, Yost immediately closed the range and the *Cape Gloucester* score climbed to three before the paint was barely dry on rising sun number two. For Colonel Yost, it raised his personal score to seven, counting the six he had shot down at Guadalcanal in December three years before.

For the rest of July, things returned largely to quiet monotony for the *Cape*. On 28 July, there was the promise of livelier action when an air strike was mounted against enemy activities in the Saddle and Parker Islands, about sixty miles southeast of Shanghai. However, instead of the reported enemy shipping, the strike found nothing but a few Chinese junks in the area. Not a bomb was dropped nor a round fired, and the disappointed pilots returned to the ship.

Beginning on 4 August, the operational tempo again picked up when 1st Lt. Thomas W. Doyle of VMF-351, on CAP, spotted a lone enemy transport moving across the area. He promptly flamed it with a short burst and rising sun number four soon appeared on the bridge, to the delight of the *Cape* and its crew. On the very next day, Colonel Yost was leading a CAP mission when a Betty bomber was detected heading for Japan. This once very common enemy aircraft had become a rarity at this stage of the war, and the CAG was determined to make it his number eight. He closed rapidly and a short burst was all that was needed as it exploded and fell into the sea. That was rising sun number five for *Cape Gloucester* and its last score for World War II, as it turned out.

On 6 August, MCVG-4 mounted its last strike of the war. Reconnaissance photos taken the day before by 1st Lt. Robert E. Benton and 2d Lts. William A. Naylon and Robert J. R. Pundt of VMF-351 revealed some very interesting activity at Tinghai in the Parker Island group. The photos showed an operating airfield, a seaplane base, and antiaircraft positions. Without delay, in company with the air groups of *Lunga Point* (CVE 94) and *Makin Island* (CVE 93), MCVG-4 attacked with rockets and strafing. A gun position was destroyed, several others silenced, one AKA sunk, and shops at the seaplane ramp heavily damaged. The Marines suffered no losses although three fighters were hit by flak. Major McLean, the VMF(CVS)-351 skipper, was hit in the belly tank and the bottom of the fuselage; Lieutenant Pundt had his belly tank knocked off; and 2d Lt. Joseph F. Carraher had his belly tank and antenna shot off. Fortunately, all three returned safely to the ship without further incident even though it was a hard day for belly tanks.

These pictures were taken by *Block Island* and *Gilbert Islands* pilots at Formosa immediately after the enemy surrendered. *Above:* a flock of Bettys and Sallys; *below:* a horde of Vals.

On 7 August, the ship returned to Okinawa and moored in Buckner Bay, where the crew received news of the atomic bomb drop at Hiroshima. The last week of the war for *Cape Gloucester* was spent there in the same spot in Buckner Bay, making the nights particularly harrowing as the enemy tried to get his last kamikaze attacks in before the end. Luckily the *Cape* was not hit, although she was only a short distance away from *Pennsylvania* (BB 38) when the battleship took an aerial torpedo and suffered over twenty fatalities. Remarkably, *Pennsylvania* had been hit at Pearl Harbor at the beginning of the war and was also the last heavy unit hit by the enemy.

On 10 August (local date), a second atomic bomb was dropped on Nagasaki and on the fifteenth the war officially was ended with the Japanese surrender. The fifteenth was also the date of *Vella Gulf*'s arrival at Okinawa with MCVG-3, the fourth and last of the Marine CVE air groups to reach the combat zones of World War II. Glad as all hands were that the war had ended, it was something of a disappointment to MCVG-3 nevertheless. Under the command of Lt. Col. Royce W. Coln, another Solomons veteran, the air group had trained hard to the same combat standards as its three predecessors. VMF(CVS)-513, under Lt. Col. Thomas O. Bales, and VMTB (CVS)-234, commanded by Capt. Edward J. Montagne, had prepared the two squadrons well.

It was a further frustration upon arrival at Guam to find orders for the air group to operate ashore at Marpi Point in Saipan while *Vella Gulf* was diverted to ferry replacement aircraft to Okinawa. MCVG-3 flew back aboard the ship off Guam five days later. It was not the best way to wind up a very intensive training period of several months, although all hands were delighted with the prospect of an early return home.

Block Island and *Gilbert Islands* were assigned together once more in mid-September, after the cessation of hostilities. Under Colonel Cooley, the two ships were involved with the re-

In the summer of 1945 1st Lt. Carroll R. "Moose" Vogelaar shows
some of his squadron mates how an enemy pilot ended his war.

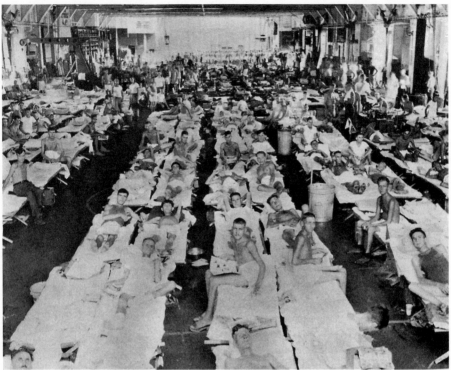

British, Australian, and New Zealand prisoners of war are housed on the hangar deck of *Block Island*. They were transported from POW camps on Formosa on the initial leg of their trip home after many years in Japanese custody.

patriation of allied prisoners of war from the POW camps in Formosa. Colonel Cooley was also assigned to take the surrender of the enemy forces based on Formosa. It was an interesting assignment and was carried out without any complicating incidents. The POWs, largely Australian, New Zealand, and British troops, were generally in very poor condition, but were overjoyed to see the American Marines.

All four Marine CVEs were involved with similar movements of Allied POWs or shifts of American troops in the immediate post-hostilities period. A single photo of the hangar deck of *Block Island* shows a few aspects of one of these assignments.

Vella Gulf and its air group were involved with antisubmarine patrols and general surveillance missions off the Japanese coast in September, where they encountered some rough weather in "typhoon territory." On 24 September, the ship was ordered to Okinawa to pick up 650 troops for return to the States. It was a happy, but crowded mission. The troops were all billeted on the hangar deck, and as a result air operations were not included as part of the trip. At Hawaii all MCVG-3 aircraft were unloaded for further disposition. The Marines debarked at Alameda, California, for further transport to Santa Barbara for demobilization.

At the end of the war, it may be said that the Marine CVE program was proceeding well along the lines laid down by Admiral King. The objective was to have eight MCVGs participating in support of Marine Corps ground forces in the November assault of Kyushu. At V-J Day, four MCVGs were well established with their carriers, fully trained and deployed to the combat area. Several follow-on MCVGs were in various states of training at Santa Barbara and Mojave, with two having already reported to their assigned CVEs and very close to readiness to deploy.

Without doubt the most important factor of the Marine CVE program was the establishment of a precedent that future Marine Corps amphibious operations could best be supported by Marine aviation units operating from carriers. The concept was given substantial "proofing" a short five years after V-J Day, when Marine squadrons were in very effective support of the 1st Marine Brigade from two CVEs off the Pusan perimeter in Korea. Further substantial conceptual verification was also found in the same CVE force operating in support of the 1st Marine Division landings at Inchon a short time later.

While ship types change with technological advances in weapons systems, the concept of supporting Marine ground forces from carriers in the amphibious assault remains established today. The World War II operations of both the ten VMFs aboard the fast carriers and the MCVGs aboard the CVEs helped immeasurably in setting precedents that are very much a part of naval and Marine aviation today, five decades later.

Carrier Operations, World
War II Style

Operations from aircraft carriers have always had a higher intrinsic risk than those from land bases. This was particularly true in the case of the straight-deck carriers of World War II. For example, with both landing and parked aircraft on the same axis, the inherent hazards in the design of these ships can readily be seen. Post–World War II developments have reduced the comparative risk factor, but it is still there.

The approach to the carrier, as directed by the ship, would normally be by a division of four aircraft executing a "break" over the ship to the downwind leg. The aircraft would take interval on the downwind leg while adjusting speed, attitude, and altitude in preparation for the landing approach. With landing gear and tailhook down and the aircraft set for landing, the individual approach would commence when opposite the island structure of the ship.

The approach would start with a shallow left turn flown 3 to 5 knots above the aircraft's stalling speed and at an altitude about 100 to 150 feet above the water. The turn would be flown through 180 degrees right up to the ship where, if all were still correct, the LSO (landing signal officer) would signal the cut. At the cut, the pilot would smartly retard the throttle to idle, level the wings, align the aircraft with the centerline of the flight deck, ease the back pressure on the stick, and land aboard. With the aircraft speed so close to stall, all these simultaneous actions achieved minimum forward speed in a three-point attitude, permitting the extended hook to engage an arresting cable.

This approach pattern to straight-deck carriers was dictated by necessary accommodations to several factors. Prominent among them was the standard configuration of the propeller-driven aircraft of the day. To provide clearance for the propeller, the aircraft design solution was a "tail down" three-point attitude of the aircraft at rest. As propellers grew in length and engines grew in size, the nose of the single-engine, high-performance aircraft became longer to provide the necessary clearance. The resulting obstructions to pilot vision when flying "low and slow" in a nose-high attitude had to be accommodated. This dictated the approach described, permitting the pilot to keep the ship and LSO up the aircraft and begin his signals at about the 90-degree point of the approach turn.

The LSO platform was immediately behind a retractable canvas wind screen. He gave his semaphore-like signals to the aircraft with two "paddles," which were slotted for low wind resistance and ease of handling. The paddles were made of highly visible materials for the earliest possible pickup by the approaching aircraft.

Post–World War II improvements in carrier design have

eliminated many of the approach pattern dictates of the straight-deck carriers. The flight decks today are much larger and have an angled landing area, which eliminates the hazards of the straight deck parking area. The numbers, types, and capabilities of aircraft-handling equipment available have brought greater flexibility to operations. The angled deck, the improved arresting gear, the optical landing system, and the steam catapults have together solved a host of problems. With the electronic advances in navigation and communications and the high-performance jet aircraft of today, carrier pilots lead a less demanding and a safer life than their World War II predecessors.

121 ■

Carrier
Operations,
World
War II
Style

Tactical Air Force
Organization at Okinawa

As 1 April, "L-day" for the Okinawa landings, drew closer, a tremendous sense of participation was brought to Marine aviation "across the board." The Marine III Amphibious Corps (IIIAC), under the command of Maj. Gen. Roy S. Geiger (the 1st Marine Air Wing [MAW] commander at Guadalcanal), comprised half the Tenth U.S. Army, which was to be the assault landing force. The IIIAC was composed of two Marine divisions, the 1st and the 6th. The Tenth Army was supported by a strong tactical air force (TAF) under the command of Maj. Gen. Francis P. Mulcahy, who was also the commanding general of the 2d MAW, as he had been in the Solomons.

The composition of the TAF as set forth by Robert Sher-rod in his famed *History of Marine Corps Aviation in World War II* is indicative of the prestige and acclaim of Marine air, afloat and ashore, earned in almost four years of the war to that time. Mulcahy's command was an impressive joint air force. At the outset it had two Marine aircraft groups totaling six day- and two night-fighter squadrons. In May and early June, two more Marine air groups were added, bringing the total Marine strength to twelve day- and three night-fighter squadrons.

From mid-May to mid-June, the 301st Army Air Force Fighter Wing was in place, adding nine day- and one night-fighter squadrons to the total. Together with five Marine air warning squadrons and four Army air warning and control organizations, all fighter units were placed under the Air Defense Command. It was commanded by Marine Brig. Gen. William J. Wallace, initial air defense commander at Guadalcanal. It was a large part of the joint TAF with a very large job to do in keeping the kamikazes off the many elements of the invasion force, ashore and afloat.

Today's reader must bear in mind that although the battle for Okinawa was primarily fought on the island, it also reached out to considerable distances within the surrounding waters. In order to protect the ships servicing the landed forces, air defense responsibilities operated outward substantially from the island. A destroyer picket line that provided early radar detection of incoming raids, for example, reached out as much as fifty to sixty miles from the island coastline in the directions of the most probable incoming threats. Small CAPs were stationed over the picket ships as often as possible in order to provide them ready air defense against kamikaze attack. If feasible, whenever an attack on a radar picket ship developed, its CAP would be augmented as quickly as possible.

The TAF functional responsibilities also included task units covering antisubmarine warfare (two Marine torpedo squadrons), photographic reconnaissance (Army), and air support control (Marines). From late June to early July, an Army bomber command was added to the TAF. It consisted of sixteen squadrons in four separate bomber groups: two heavy, one medium, and one light. Strategic bombing responsibilities for the B-29s resided in higher command areas such as Headquarters Army Air Forces and CinCPac.

For the Okinawa operation the TAF was the organization that was the centerpiece for reuniting Marine air with Marine ground forces. It was a long separation, with very few exceptions, covering a stretch of many months from the end of the Solomons campaign to the start of the Okinawa assault. The TAF brought not only the seaborne Marine fighter squadrons of Task Forces 38 and 58, but also those Marine air units that had done so much in support of the Army in the Philippines, into support of the Marine divisions on Okinawa. Before Okinawa had progressed very far, the first three Marine aircraft groups of the newly approved Marine CVE program also came briefly to the support of their ground brethren under TAF control. It was entirely fitting that the whole reunion of Marine air and ground came to pass under a prestigious joint air command headed by a Marine aviator.

125 ∎

Tactical
Air Force
Organiza-
tion at
Okinawa

Marine Pilots in the
Navy Squadrons of Task
Forces 38 and 58

In the complexities of something as cataclysmic
and all-encompassing as World War II, some very unusual
administrative events inevitably occur. Marine aviation by
1945 had reached a total number of pilots in excess of ten
thousand. This record would be incomplete without an ac-
count of the Marine pilots in *Intrepid* (CV 11) and *Shangri-La*
(CV 38).

The "*Intrepid* Marines" came into being in late March 1945.
When the *Wasp* air group, with VMF-216 and VMF-217, arrived at Guam homeward bound after completing their tour
on the front lines, 1st Lt. George A. Krumm and three other
pilots were transferred to replacement pool CVEs. From the

Attu (CVE 102), the four were assigned to *Intrepid.* They went aboard understanding that "the *Intrepid* Marine squadrons needed some replacements." When they reported aboard, however, they found that the carrier had no Marine squadrons—only Navy. Nevertheless, they were told that if they could fly Corsairs, VF-10 "had some openings." VF-10 was the F4F "Grim Reaper" squadron that had become famous at the Battle of Midway and in many other engagements of 1942 and 1943. The four Marines signed up immediately as a Marine fighter division. A week later, 1st Lt. William A. Nickerson brought aboard another Marine four-plane division from the replacement pool in response to the original formal request by *Intrepid* for replacements. They too were accepted by VF-10, making a Marine detachment of eight.

Although their "hiring" by VF-10 only lasted until *Intrepid* took a kamikaze two weeks later, the unusual detachment made its presence felt. Lieutenants Krumm and Nickerson were each credited with three enemy aircraft and 1st Lts. Harry O. Taylor and Hugh F. Newell with two apiece. All told, the *Intrepid* Marines qualified as bona fide Grim Reapers. Unfortunately, there is always a price to pay, and this case was no exception. The sharpshooters of Ishigaki brought down 2d Lt. Carl R. Miller on 5 April and he was not seen again.

The *Shangri-La* Marines had an even more interesting twist to their history. It all started with orders for two second lieutenant pilots of VMF(CVS)-512 at Santa Barbara to proceed at once by Pan American clipper to Hawaii. This was a mode of wartime expedited transport for urgent changes and was normally reserved for more senior officers. Nevertheless, 2d Lts. Morris W. Hitson and Joseph Januszewski reported to MCAS Ewa, where they promptly qualified in landings aboard carriers in the area. They were then sent to Guam, where they flew for several days with VMF-215 before being ordered to Saipan for assignment to Navy Bomber Fighter Squadron 99 at Marpi Point. Three additional Marines joined them at VBF-99 to make up one fighter division, "plus one spare."

The five replacement Marines requalified on board one of the carriers operating in the area. Shortly thereafter the five were ordered to *Bougainville* (CVE 100), a floating replacement pool for the fast carriers. En route to the fleet off Okinawa, *Bougainville* was damaged in a typhoon and the wandering Marines were transferred, via a destroyer, to *Shangri-La* and Navy Air Group 99. CVG-99 was close to finishing a three-month period of operations against kamikaze bases in the region, and for the next two weeks, the *Shangri-La* Marines were a daily part of that.

About 20 June, *Shangri-La* set course for Leyte Gulf for a well-earned period of rest and replenishment. On arrival the Marines saw *Gilbert Islands* and MCVG-2, their "old home" moored nearby. Since they sensed that their newly found Navy shipmates were about to be relieved, they visited MCVG-2 to see what the "prospects" of a transfer might be. Colonel Campbell was agreeable, and they all joined VMF (CVS)-512 shortly before it departed to support the Australian landing at Balikpapan.

No matter how these events came to pass, at this point fifty years later one has to admire the ingenuity and initiative that were involved.

Index

Italicized numbers indicate an illustration on that page.

About the Author

Maj. Gen. John P. Condon, U.S. Naval Academy Class of 1934, earned his wings in 1937. He served on active duty from 31 May 1934 to 1 October 1962, holding command positions at squadron, group, and wing levels. General Condon served in World War II, in the Korean War, and the War in Vietnam. After retiring from the Marine Corps, General Condon worked in industry from 1963 to 1977 and as a volunteer historian at the Marine Corps Historical Center from 1979 until his death in December 1996. He was a charter member, past president, and chairman of the Marine Corps Historical Foundation. General Condon received a B.S. at the Naval Academy and his M.S. and Ph.D. at the University of California at Irvine. He also studied at the U.S. Air Force's Air War College in 1950 and was selected for the Marine Corps' Advanced Research Group (Quantico) in 1953. His essays have been published in the *Marine Corps Gazette*, the U.S. Naval Institute's *Proceedings* magazine, and the Naval Aviation Museum Foundation magazine, *Foundation*.

The NAVAL INSTITUTE PRESS is the book-publishing arm of the U.S. Naval Institute, a private, nonprofit, membership society for sea service professionals and others who share an interest in naval and maritime affairs. Established in 1873 at the U.S. Naval Academy in Annapolis, Maryland, where its offices remain today, the Naval Institute has members worldwide.

Members of the Naval Institute support the education programs of the society and receive the influential monthly magazine *Proceedings* and discounts on fine nautical prints and on ship and aircraft photos. They also have access to the transcripts of the Institute's Oral History Program and get discounted admission to any of the Institute-sponsored seminars offered around the country.

The Naval Institute also publishes *Naval History* magazine. This colorful bimonthly is filled with entertaining and thought-provoking articles, first-person reminiscences, and dramatic art and photography. Members receive a discount on *Naval History* subscriptions.

The Naval Institute's book-publishing program, begun in 1898 with basic guides to naval practices, has broadened its scope in recent years to include books of more general interest. Now the Naval Institute Press publishes about 100 titles each year, ranging from how-to books on boating and navigation to battle histories, biographies, ship and aircraft guides, and novels. Institute members receive discounts of 20 to 50 percent on the Press's nearly 600 books in print.

Full-time students are eligible for special half-price membership rates. Life memberships are also available.

For a free catalog describing Naval Institute Press books currently available, and for further information about subscribing to *Naval History* magazine or about joining the U.S. Naval Institute, please write to:

MEMBERSHIP DEPARTMENT
U.S. Naval Institute
118 Maryland Avenue
Annapolis, MD 21402-5035

Telephone: (800) 233-8764
Fax: (410) 279-7940
Web address: www.usni.org